THE CRAFT OF
COPYWRITING

To Jill

THE CRAFT OF COPYWRITING

by Alastair Crompton

Published in association with
THE CAM FOUNDATION
(Communication, Advertising and
Marketing Education Foundation)

BUSINESS BOOKS
COMMUNICA - EUROPA

First published 1979

© ALASTAIR CROMPTON 1979

ISBN   0 220 67006 4 (Case bound)
          0 220 67009 9 (Limp bound)

This book has been set in 11 on 12pt Baskerville
Printed by Thomson Litho Ltd., East Kilbride, Scotland
Bound by Hunter & Foulis, Edinburgh.
For the publishers, Business Books Limited,
24 Highbury Crescent, London N.5

CONTENTS

Foreword by David Abbott   *ix*
Preface   *xi*

Chapter 1   **Your first day in the creative department**   *1*
               The personnel in an advertising agency —
               Account people — Media people —
               Production people — The creative
               director — Copywriters — Art directors —
               Typographers — The studio manager —
               Illustrators — Finished artists — Paste-up
               artists

Chapter 2   **The creative director**   *10*
               His job — When he should produce ads —
               His work as a presenter — New business
               pitches — Administration — Control of
               the work-flow — Distribution of accounts
               — Discipline in the department — Credit
               where credit is due — Hiring — Firing —
               Grooming a successor — Relations with
               Headhunters — Quality control — The
               most difficult job in the agency

Chapter 3   **Good habits to get into**   *19*
               How to start work — The medium and
               how to use it — The size of space and

v

how to use it — How magazines can tell
you about your audience — Copy dates —
The use of bleed — The product and how
to find out about it: from the maker and
from the user — How to work with an
art director — How to maintain a good
relationship — The practical steps to
making an ad — The 'over-night test'

Chapter 4   **There are only two kinds of**   30
                advertising
                When you have something to say, say
                it — But simplify — Work for the big
                idea — Be single-minded — Rosser
                Reeves — The USP — And the US-
                personality — When you have nothing
                to say, use showmanship — Examples
                of campaigns produced when there
                was nothing to say — How to look
                beyond the product — Different kinds
                of products — A little about technique

Chapter 5   **Work on what to say, not on how to**   39
                say it
                Faults to avoid when you start to
                write — The advertising strategy — What
                it is — What it tells you — How it helps —
                The first vital question: who are you
                talking to? — The second vital question:
                what do you want to say? — A case
                history — Practical steps that can lead
                to ideas

Chapter 6   **Some techniques**   51
                How people read advertisements — What
                that can teach you — How to write
                headlines — Captions — Slogans — Body
                copy — The subjects that make people
                read — Copy the editor — The WHY
                technique — The HOW technique — The

WHERE technique — The WHO
technique — The WHEN technique

Chapter 7   **More techniques**   67
Before and after — Invent a place —
Invent a character/s — Put the client in
the ad — Give the product a second
name — Comparison advertising — The
challenge — The guarantee — Torture
tests — When words collide — Games
with the alphabet — The 'buzz' words

Chapter 8   **Still more techniques**   80
Contests — Testimonials — Topical
advertising — Quizzes and tests — Range
advertising — Quotations — Demonstration — Show and tell — Slice of life —
Trick film — Animation — The 'day'
idea — Strip cartoons

Chapter 9   **Television**   93
How TV *makes* the viewer view — When
to use TV — When to avoid TV — The
basic rules of scriptwriting — Case
history — Sound versus pictures — TV
for demonstrating — Name campaigns —
The presenter commercial — Jingles —
How to use personalities — Voice-over —
Press versus TV

Chapter 10   **Talking to the housewife**   103
How to talk to women — The importance
of facts and information — Intelligent
argument for a product — Subjects that
make women read — Pictures that pull —
Recipes — Coupons — Free samples —
Scratch and sniff — Economy packs —
Value for money — The beauty business
— Dotting the "i's"

Chapter 11   **How to judge your work**   *114*
The seven silver rules of making ads —
Is it on strategy? — Is it clear who you're
talking to? — Is your ad interesting? —
Is your ad instant? — Is your ad
believable? — Is your ad unexpected? —
Have you proved your case? — How these
rules can help sell your work

Chapter 12   **How to defend your work**   *123*
The hurdles every ad has to jump —
The creative director's OK — The
account people — The plans board —
The client (at all levels) — Common
criticisms and sensible answers —
Criticisms you should heed — Don't
fight for bad work

Chapter 13   **How to present your work**   *135*
Why the team that did the work should
present it — When you most have the
client's ear — How to prepare for a
presentation — Scripts versus storyboards — The role of the strategy in
presentations — Test commercials —
Thinking on your feet — The 'surprise'
element — How to end the presentation

Chapter 14   **How to live with a dead compaign**   *145*
Why campaigns are rejected — How to
maintain good relations with the client —
Never write the old campaign with new
words — The role of creative director
here — Picking brains — Reviewing the
media — How to cope with time problems
— What *not* to do — There is always
another campaign — What makes a
professional copywriter

Index   *157*

FOREWORD

by David Abbott
*Creative Director and Partner
of Abbott, Mead, Davies & Vickers Limited*

When Alastair showed me the manuscript for this book and asked me to write the foreword to it, I felt both pleased and aged. I knew by this flattering request that I had finally reached the status of elder statesman only a few months before reaching my 40th birthday.

Such reflections caused me to think back to my own beginnings as a copywriter. I started in the days when advertising was still a refuge for the gifted amateur. At my first agency, a famous poet had the office to the right of me and a part-time novelist paid the rent by appearing three days a week in the office to my left. I used to feel their ambiguity seeping through the walls.

Fortunately, in my own office, there were several established writers who loved the craft of copywriting. For them it was not a substitute form of writing. They took pride in their craft and passed on to me their knowledge and their enthusiasm. I have been indebted to them ever since and I fancy many young writers will feel the same way about Alastair after reading this book.

It is a practical book, the lessons he passes on have been learnt first hand, yet it fairly bubbles with enthusiasm. To enjoy success as a copywriter you must enjoy copywriting. Like all good teachers, Alastair passes on his own love for his subject and, in the end, that might be the most valuable lesson in this valuable book.

PREFACE

This book is written for anyone who wants to know how advertisements are made. You may be a student taking a course in advertising. You may be at university, wondering whether a writing job in an advertising agency is something you could, or would like, to do. You may have already joined an agency as a trainee, and want to know a little about the creative side of the business. You may be a young copywriter who wonders if this book has anything to tell him.

You may be an established copywriter interested in how a colleague sees the business. You may be a brand manager, keen to understand better the creative work presented to you. Or you may have nothing to do with advertising at all and are just trying to find out if there is any truth in the talk about hidden persuaders and mind manipulating, and whether there are secret techniques used to sell the public goods it doesn't want, at prices it can't afford.

If you are any of those people, you'll get something from this book. Its special aim, however, is to turn would-be copywriters into very good copywriters who will find themselves in demand and able to earn a good living. If it means that more people produce intelligent advertising, and more companies get better value for money from their agencies, or if it helps you be happy and make money in the job you have chosen to do, it will have been worthwhile.

Note on the illustrations

As a copywriter, I may have been heard to say that the most important part of any advertisement is the headline. But the advertisements reproduced in this book (which show work from some of London's best agencies) have been included because of their pictures. (This is why I have given the art directors a credit, but not the various copywriters.)

In every case, the picture improves the headline. In many cases the picture is doing more than half the work of the whole advertisement. In some cases, without the picture, the headline would be either banal or make no sense.

When you first begin to learn the craft of copywriting, you tend to think that it is the words which should carry the brunt of the sales pitch. The advertisements shown here demonstrate it isn't always so. They also demonstrate another point: a headline which says only what you can see from the picture, is working at half strength.

I have not set out to pick the best ads of the decade. Some of the work included has been commended by the judges of creative work, but most of it has passed without any recognition from any award-giving body. Yet every ad is an excellent piece of craftsmanship that has earned its place here because it can teach you something. So when you come to them, look at the advertisements to see what techniques they use, because it is by understanding those that you will help yourself to do better work.

A.C.

Chapter 1

YOUR FIRST DAY IN THE CREATIVE DEPARTMENT

Advertising agencies need four kinds of people: account people, media people, production people and creative people. The first three kinds have no place in this book, although you will find them wandering in and out of its pages. But we can't have you sitting in your office the first day without knowing who is likely to walk in, so let us begin with the briefest description of what account, media and production people do.

Account people are the ones with nice suits, nice haircuts and nice accents. Their job is to represent the agency to the client, and the client to the agency. They help the client to think through every aspect of selling his product. They carry reports of the client's needs to the agency and they carry the work the agency produces to the client. They are, in a word, the contact people. Of course, a good account person is primarily a businessman able to understand and make recommendations on every aspect of selling. Generally speaking, it is an account person who is the chairman or managing director of the agency.

You're unlikely to start work on any advertisement unless you have first been briefed by an account person. An account person knows the client, understands his business, and should have virtually all the facts about it at his fingertips. Account people want to be loved, they want creative people to be able to think clearly and work very fast, and they do not want to be shouted at. You will be a more successful copy-writer if you learn to like them.

Media people also wear nice suits, but they are occasionally seen with their jackets and ties off. It is their job to know all about, and tell you all about, newspapers, television, magazines, posters and radio, in fact, any medium where your advertisement could appear. They should know who reads, looks at and listens to the various media and how you can reach the most people the most often and most effectively for the least money. Sometimes media people can be very imaginative; if you find an imaginative media person, grapple him to thy soul with hoops of steel. He can make an idea you have communicate better and faster simply by suggesting the appropriate medium for it.

Production people do not always wear nice suits and are frequently seen in sweaters, T-shirts or sports jackets and jeans. This in no way affects their efficiency; in fact, it has been argued that the more relaxed they are in their dress, the better they are able to concentrate on the job they have to do. This argument is also put forward to explain why creative prople often look very scruffy.

The production person's job is to take the advertisement you have made and handle it in such a way that it can be reproduced on a poster or in a newspaper or magazine. Production people understand what will and will not look good when it is printed, and should be listened to if they tell you that your advertisement is going to look a disaster. They will advise you how small you can make a photograph before it becomes indecipherable on coarse newsprint. They will chat to printers and encourage them to reproduce faithfully the colours in a transparency. They are happy to make suggestions on what should be retouched in order to print with clarity.

In my experience, production people are willing and cheerful, and if you speak to them as colleagues there is little they will not do for you. They also have access to a stream of weekly and monthly magazines which often reach their offices before they reach the bookstalls, and for copies of which your wife will be very grateful. Copywriters should never get on the wrong side of production people because they rely on them for the proofs of their work which go to make up a writer's portfolio.

The creative types

Now you know the three kinds of people (apart from creative people) who, if you have landed in a friendly agency, might knock on your door and introduce themselves, it is time to talk about creative people. The creative person who will be closest to you every day of your working life will be your art director. An art director, as the name suggests, directs the way an advertisement looks. He lays it out, decides what should be in the picture, supervises the photograph or drawing if there is one, decides on the appropriate type-face, the size and positioning of the logotype (client's name block), and how big the body text should be. You may work solely with one art director, or you may work with several on different accounts, depending on the system operating in your agency. It doesn't really matter, so long as you actually *work with* an art director. There was a time when copywriters sat in one department, wrote their words, then sent them through the messenger boy to the art directors sitting in another department. The problem with this was that it overlooked the simple fact that two heads are better than one. Two creative people working to make an advertisement are likely to make it quicker and better if they swop headlines and ideas. So although you may have an office of your own, you should always be willing to leave it and join your art director in his office. If you are both sitting together anyway, so much the better, although there are some writers who prefer a cubbyhole to themselves as (they say) it helps them to think about the body text of their advertisement and bash away on their typewriters without disturbing anyone.

There are other kinds of creative people besides art directors, and one you should get to know early is the television producer. A good TV and film producer is worth his weight in gold medals. Even if you choose the production company and director you want to make the film, the agency producer, if he is doing his job properly, will help you make sure that the idea you have in your mind is the one that ends up on the screen. He will also be able to tell you, if you have a wild, crazy idea, whether it is practicable. He will know at first glance whether your script contains too many words for the length of film, or radio commercial. If he is a professional, he will be able to 'see' the commercial before it is made, and know whether it's going to work or not.

The television producer also takes care of all the boring but important details of TV work. He OKs the bills, books the artists, reserves recording studios, plans trips if you're off on location, and does a dozen things that if they weren't looked after would spell disaster. Make friends with your television producer and do not get on your high horse if he dares to comment on your scripts. He may not be able to write them himself, any more than you can write, say, a pop song, but he should be allowed a view as to whether he likes them or not.

The typographer

Another creative person who'll help you is the agency typographer, the man who knows how best to suit the typeface to the message. He's the man who, to take an extreme example, if your headline says GIVE A DAMN, will not let you set it in script, or if it says ANGELS OF MERCY, is unlikely to recommend a heavy black sans serif face. He can also tell you how much room a given number of words will take up. He will recommend complimentary faces, so that the body text does not look out of place with the headline. He will help with adaptations to larger or smaller spaces. And if you take him to lunch and get him talking, he's likely to spellbind you with stories about the history of type.

If you are lucky, your agency will have an illustrator. He's the person who takes your advertisement after you've thought of it and draws it up so you can present it to the client. The one thing he must be able to do is draw, but the best illustrators should also be able to read your mind; and if you want the baby in the picture to have a particular smile, or the housewife to have a certain expression, he should be able to capture it for you. It calls for a deftness of touch and a skill to create impressions without overworking the picture and the best illustrators soon leave advertising agencies and work freelance because they can earn a lot more money. Illustrators may also decide to become art directors and thereby enjoy the thrill of initiating ideas, while illustrators have to interpret the ideas of other people.

The chief and the indians

There are two other kinds of creative people we haven't yet talked about: the creative director and the people who do the finished artwork in the agency studio. The creative director you will have already met. He's the one who interviewed you and gave you the job. His role is one of the most important in the agency and because, if you are a good writer, you may one day be a creative director yourself, I have given him a chapter to himself. The studio manager and the paste-up artists are also worth making friends with. Their job is to liaise with the production people, preparing the finished artwork so that your advertisements can be printed. They need patience, a sense of design and a keen eye, and if they do their job properly, they can save the agency a lot of money and you a lot of heartache. If they do their job badly, they can lose everyone a fortune.

Don't just sit there, do something

Right, there you are sitting at your desk, and you know who might come and visit you. What do you need before you can start work? You need a chair you feel comfortable in, pulled up to a desk you feel comfortable at. You need a layout pad and some thin and thick felt-tip pens. You need a typewriter and typing paper. Some copywriters say that they cannot work straight onto a typewriter. First they can't type and, secondly, they find the habit of writing in longhand helps

5

them think, and lets them go back to cross words out without the palaver of pushing reverse keys. If you haven't made up your mind one way or the other, my advice is to work *with* a typewriter. The fact that you find it hard to type to start with will make you think twice about every word before you put it down. Gradually, you will get the feel of the number of words you have written and this will help you economise on words and avoid going on too long. And lastly, you won't have to stand over your secretary when she is typing the finished version, apologising for your terrible writing. But I should make it clear that the typewriter doesn't come into the act until you are writing the body copy. And before that, you and the art director must have thought of the theme and pictures which will make up the advertisement. In other words, you have to have had the idea.

Most young copywriters also start off with three books: a dictionary, Roget's *Thesaurus,* and a dictionary of quotations. A straight dictionary I agree is essential, but in all my time as a copywriter, I can't remember a single occasion when Roget or the dictionary of quotations were of any help whatever. Neither of them ever gave me the faintest advertising idea.

Where you *will* get a lot of help, however, is from the agency library. (If your agency hasn't got one, then spend 10 minutes on the streets until you've found the nearest public library). Introduce yourself to the person in charge, and let them know you are a copywriter and you have to produce advertisements, and to do that you can never have too many facts. And that you intend to be in and out of the library, checking and finding out things, for as long as you belong to the agency. Good library people are never happier than when their resources are being stretched, and provided you always return stuff they lend you, you'll never have a problem.

A good agency library has a section on statistics where you should be able to find out facts like how many airlines or railways there are in the world, how many people in Birmingham own colour televisions, and so on. It also, generally, has a set of *Encyclopaedia Brittanicas* which have many times provided the spice that made my body copy appetising. I once had the job of writing 10 consecutive half-page advertisements in a magazine, each one featuring a bottle of fizzy mixer drink (tonic, ginger ale, soda, and so on). It was clear to me that I could never fill 10 half-pages with interesting stuff about mixers; on the other hand, stories and lore about drinking have filled books. A few minutes in the library and I found the reminiscences of the head barman of a top hotel. There was enough meat there to make 10 half-pages relevant and riveting.

Go to the pictures

The next thing you should do is phone up the agency cinema and ask them to show you the house reel. The house reel, for those who don't know, is a selection of the latest film and television commercials the agency has produced, and of which it is most proud. It is most frequently wheeled out and shown to prospective clients when the agency is pitching for new business. Watching the house reel will do two things: first, get you familiar with the clients in the agency who use the cinema or TV, and, secondly, show you the general standard of agency creative work to give you an idea what you have to live up to.

If you haven't already got one, you should get a list of *all* the clients the agency has. You will almost certainly have been told those clients whose accounts you will be expected to work on. Go to the production manager and ask if you can borrow the guard books of your accounts. The guard books (again for those who don't know) contain a record of every newspaper and magazine advertisement that has ever been prepared for that particular company while it has been a client of your agency. It is a potted history of that company's advertising. You can have an enjoyable time just following the various themes which have been used, and they should, ideally, have one overall tone of voice which you will have to emulate before you are able to carry on the good work.

A lot of good agencies also keep a track of the advertising done by their clients' main competitors. That too is worth digging out, provided you are careful not to be daunted by the mass of ideas that have already been tried. For every campaign theme that's ever seen the light of day, there are two more waiting to be born. And if you are wondering if any of them are ever going to strike you, you've come to the right place, because that's mostly what this book is about.

Finally, a word about your fellow copywriters. Naturally, they'll want to meet you and they'll ask you what accounts you have been given to try your skills on. Mostly this can be a pleasant and useful interchange of views, but on one point you should be very careful, and that is, do try not to pick up any of your compatriots' pre-conceived views. There's nothing worse than when someone hears you are working on Brand X, to be told: 'Oh you poor sod, that's a terrible account. They never buy anything good'. Properly translated, that means: 'I'm glad I got rid of that account, because I never did anything good on it'.

Don't knock it if you haven't tried it

I have known accounts which had such terrible reputations that it was very hard persuading any creative person in the agency to work on them. Then one day, a new guy arrives, and they pass this so-called terrible account to him. Soon people begin to notice that the account is getting better and that the client is beginning to accept good work. And it isn't too long before it becomes a coveted account with quite a few people willing to work on it. What happened was that the new guy who joined knew that there were no such things as terrible accounts; there are simply terrible people working on them. I once got my hands on a single account worth over a million pounds – the largest appropriation I have ever handled in my life. My mouth watered as I imagined the ads that kind of money made possible. After my third campaign hadn't got past the account controller's office, I still swore that it wasn't a terrible account. It was simply terribly handled. The client was being defrauded of value for money, had been badly advised and badly served for years, and when attempts were made to break that vicious circle, they were stamped on because the account people 'knew what the client wanted'. Situations like this always end the same sad way. One day the account switches to a new agency that has prepared *a revolutionary new campaign,* and even as the first new ad appears you can hear the account people who lost the business saying: 'But that's not what they want'. Happily, the great majority of account people are only too pleased if they get some fresh thinking on the account, provided only that it is apposite. So be careful how your attitude towards your new place is coloured. If you can put on your coat at going home time, sure in the knowledge that you haven't picked up even the faintest whiff of disappointment about any of the accounts you have been asked to look after, believe me, you've done a good day's work.

Chapter 2

THE CREATIVE DIRECTOR

The chair behind the desk in the creative director's office is reckoned by many to be the hot-seat of the agency. Creative directors leave agencies more often than managing directors, financial directors, media directors or even common or garden account directors who have seats on the board. Which is strange when you think how many of these there are, compared with the number of creative directors. Why should this be so? Is it that creative people are more temperamental, or more unstable, or have more itchy feet than the others? Is it that there are so few good creative directors that they are constantly being offered higher-paid, more enticing posts? Or is it that the creative director's job *is* the hardest job in the agency?

You will find agency people who subscribe to all these reasons. I have a simpler explanation. The creative director is the one man in the agency whose job it is *easy to assess*. If the agency often produces outstanding creative work, wins new accounts and retains its clients for long spells, then it can be safely assumed that the creative director is doing what is expected of him. If, on the other hand, the creative work is average to indifferent, if the agency has difficulty pulling in new accounts, and if clients complain more and more about the service they get, the place where it is easiest to *see* defects is simply by opening the nearest guard book. The work that comes out of the creative department is there for all to criticise if they wish (and when the chips are down, you'll find no shortage of critics).

Creative work is there to be seen

An account man records the decisions which have been agreed at meetings in his call reports. A media man records his decisions in media schedules. A production man has to answer when an ad reproduces less than prettily. But who reads call reports a couple of weeks after they're written? Who digs out old media schedules and scans them to see if the buying was as efficient as it might have been? The production man picks up the 'phone and blasts the printer, and maybe gets a free insertion. But the creative work is all over the walls of the agency. The whole staff sees it every day and so does every visiting or propsective client. I have actually heard people in new briefings, referring to work done previously, say, 'I hate that campaign!'. Even clients, when they become dissatisfied, are likely to take it out on the creative work first. Research done by an agency I once worked for decreed that clients moved in and out of agencies principally because of the calibre of the creative work. The ads themselves are all the general public ever sees. They are the only visible part of the agency's product. And although that product should include adventurous marketing thinking, genuinely entrepreneurial business advice, and exceptionally clever media buying, few people are in a position to judge whether all, or any, of that has been forth-coming. Yet everyone, down to the post-boy, can tell you whether the ads are any good. When trouble looms, people look for it in the nearest place, and the nearest place is where they can see it on paper and film. And if the verdict is thumbs down, then it's the creative director who is frequently under that thumb.

By now I can hear the violins playing, the tears of mock sympathy flowing, and people saying 'If you don't like the heat, get out of the kitchen'. Believe me, I'm not complaining;

11

I simply want to point out that there are times when the creative director is only as good as the last ad to come out of his department, while the account people are seldom judged on the contents of their last document. The creative director's job *is* the hardest job in the agency. Because while account people should primarily be shrewd businessmen with pleasing personalities, and creative people in the lower levels needn't have pleasant personalities so long as they produce the goods, a creative director has got to be able to write better ads than the rest of his department, be as good a business thinker as some of the best account people, have a pleasant way when he meets agency staff and clients, and be a very capable presenter. The qualifications needed for the job are pretty stiff and there are not many people who can provide them; so creative directors get very good salaries, are very much in demand, and are more easily found out if they're not up to the mark.

Don't tell me, show me

Let us consider in more detail the job of the creative director, since the lowliest creative person reading this book should, if he has any drive, eventually aspire to the post. The first requirement is that he should be able to create. The ads he makes should be the best in the agency, and the rest of his department should acknowledge they are best.

He may not make them very often, but he should be there as a long stop, so when everything else fails and the agency has to find a creative solution to a problem, he can sit down with one colleague and make a campaign that fully answers the brief. And not *just* answers the brief, but does it in a way that takes creative work to its limits in terms of originality and ingenuity, but still with a totally sound business strategy behind it. And he should only be satisfied if the rest of his department then think to themselves: 'I wish I'd done that'.

Having produced that great work, and done so in not too long a time (no client should expect to wait months for his campaign), then the creative director has to present that work. To do this he hasn't just got to be articulate with a pen in his hand. He must be able to talk clearly and concisely, and think on his feet in front of a group of people who all the time are summing up his performance. What he is saying to a client in essence is, this is how the agency believes you should spend your next half million pounds; and not only that, but if it was my own money, then this is how I would spend it myself. The techniques of presenting creative work have to be learned, and to that end I have given them a separate chapter in this book. But the very fact that I can write for a whole chapter about them should give you some idea of how complex the subject can be. Yet the best creative directors master this subject along with all the others they need at their fingertips, since there can be times when a campaign (or indeed a new account) is in the balance and that balance is tipped by a highly professional presentation. It is interesting to note that when a panel of 60 clients was asked whom they would most expect to meet at a new business presentation, without exception they included the creative director. And you don't imagine for a moment that they wouldn't very quickly sum up his abilities as a presenter. If an agency is in a new business race they are up against some of the smoothest, slickest and most impressive talkers in town. Woe betide the man who shuffles, stammers and loses the knife-like precision that lets you build a soundly reasoned argument.

All that, and more

We have agreed the creative director should be able to make the best ads and then sell them. What other attributes does he need? Obviously, he should be an efficient administrator. He should control the flow of work through the agency, allocating accounts according to the abilities of the people under him. Some will be better at television; some will be better at good sound rational argument, some will have more skill with emotional claims. The creative director must be certain every account has a creative 'mother and father'. Somebody in his department must be directly responsible for the work of each client. He must get on with the client, and be allowed as much contact with him as is sensible. So long as a creative person knows he is the *parent* of an account, you will have no trouble getting work done, and the work will generally be the best that person can produce. It's when the account has no creative parents that trouble starts. Nobody feels responsible for it, nobody wants to do it, standards quickly fall off and the account comes to be known as a 'bad' account. And as I have already emphasised, there are no such things as good or bad accounts; it's just that good or bad things have been done to them.

A creative director must be able to keep discipline. I don't mean by that that he should make the department clock-in every morning, note the times they go to lunch (and the state in which they come back) and record those days when someone knocks off half-an-hour before time. Sensible time-keeping is necessary, of course, but some of the best creative departments in the world are often empty at the peak hours of the working day. Discipline means that work is done when it is needed. And that doesn't mean five minutes before the internal review board, it means in sufficient time for revisions to be made if it is not up to standard. Discipline means that creative standards are maintained and clients get the highest calibre of creative thinking the agency can produce. And not just the giants who spend three quarters of a million or so each season, but the small companies who have fifty thousand hard-earned pounds they can afford to put into an advertising appropriation and hope to get a campaign that has an effect out of all proportion to the money they spend. Here it is important that the creative director can set the example: nothing is harder to do than ask a creative person to produce work he knows you can't produce yourself.

Know who's who and what's what

Then our man must give credit where credit is due. One writer I know has a phrase: 'Who steals my credit steals cash'. And it is true, for a good idea can win a creative person a raise in salary or even another job. I don't mean that the creative director must seek to know the origin of every slogan that ever comes before him, and search out the originator of every idea he sees. But sooner or later the people responsible for good work are recognised within the creative department itself, and the director must be sensitive enough to know when to say 'Well done' and to whom to say it, and sooner or later to discover who is pulling his weight and who is riding on the backs of his colleagues.

Another job the creative director has is to staff his department. It is difficult to tell in one interview, or even several interviews, whether the man or woman you are seeing will fit the job you have to offer. It is often hard to be sure whether he has even been responsible for all the work he is showing. There has been more than one occasion when I have been shown the same campaign by more than one creative team, each claiming responsibility for its conception. One managing director I spoke to reckoned his creative director was doing a fine job if only 50 per cent of the men he hired were any good. In this respect I acknowledge that the creative director has an easier job than a managing director, because at least the creative person has a portfolio of work and a reel of commercials by which he can be judged, while account and media people can only quote the accounts they have worked on and who is to tell whether they worked on them well or not?

The creative director needs an ear to the business grapevine so he picks up information about who around town is making the good ads. One creative director I know used to scan the papers and watch TV avidly, and when he saw work that impressed him he found out who did it, what agency they worked at, how much they were earning and, lastly, whether or not they were interested in moving. And on more than one accasion he rang them up himself to ask if they felt like a chat.

The King is dead. Long live the King

A creative director should be concerned about his successor.

When he sees a creative team steaming down the corridor with an armful of new concepts, off to present them to a client, he must be more pleased that they get along well and are gaining the confidence of their colleagues than suspicious whether they may be undermining his own position. He must encourage the people under him to take responsibility, think along the business lines he thinks along, produce work he would be happy to produce, and make decisions on those days when he is sick, or on holiday, or not around for a host of other reasons. He must appoint a deputy who, in an ideal world, is just as good as he is. He must have, beneath the deputy, a team in which he has the utmost confidence. For even in the best-organised societies, creative director's can get run over by buses, or be offered more attractive posts at more ridiculous salaries. And it is then a creative director's responsibility to say: 'John and Jean Smith are just as good at my job as I am, and when I go you can appoint them in my place with the utmost confidence. The standard of work will remain as high as it has been under my leadership and all the things you have asked me to do I know they can do. So goodbye and thank you. You may rest in confidence that I have not left you in the lurch.'

The grapevine

Those are the major functions of the creative director. He also has to do a hundred and one smaller things that no one writes into his job specifications, but which are vital if everything is to run smoothly. He must scotch nasty rumours that can arise even in the sweetest-running agencies. And to do that he must have an ear very close to the ground. Or as commonly happens he must have a discrete and loyal secretary who has an ear very close to the ground.

He must maintain a good relationship with the creative headhunters who proliferate our business, knowing when to ring them and be able to make a shrewd guess when other people in his department are ringing them. He should have good friends amongst other creative directors in town, for they can tell him very often about people he has interviewed and maybe would like to hire. He must take on the unenviable task of firing, and do it justly but delicately. He must be able to say 'no' to work without destroying the incentive of the people who did it, and instead, send them away burning with the will to do better next time. He must be able to disseminate ideas so that the people to whom he suggests them accept them in the right spirit and go away to interpret them without feeling that they will be deprived of their recognition when presenting the finished work.

Which business is the creative director's business?

He must also make up his mind about what, in my experience, is the most difficult decision of all: just how much of the work he is going to do himself. There is a temptation, especially amongst the creative directors of small and medium-sized agencies, to take the cream of the accounts — the public service campaigns and double-page spreads in the Sunday supplements — and make them himself, or with a favourite art director (for you will find that the great majority of creative directors began their careers as copywriters). In one sense this can be good, for it should mean that the prestige work the agency produces is of the highest calibre and will attract clients from outside who are looking for a change of agency. But in another sense this kind of behaviour can be very bad, for it destroys initiative. The people in the lower echelons of the department begin to feel they can stop trying, because the boss is going to have a go at the job too, and since he makes the decision which of the ads should run, there is a hundred-to-one chance that he will recommend his own. I resolved the problem very simply. I let the existing accounts in the agency go on as sweetly as they might and I put my back into new business presentations. For two reasons: one, because I believe every agency owes it to its existing clients to give them first priority as far as work is concerned, and really good work comes from the creative people who understand the account and know what the client expects from them. The second reason is that since, as creative director, I know I was expected to be in on all new business meetings and therefore should make the creative presentation myself, it ought to be my responsibility to do the work. A creative team, however conscientious, can sometimes be tempted to do less than their best if they know they are not going to be at the meeting to take the flack if anything goes wrong. I wanted to be sure when prospective clients threw bricks that they would throw them at me. Also, placed in a position of defending work, I would defend it wholeheartedly because it was *my* work. Naturally, I couldn't do all the new business pitches, and then the teams who made the ads made the presentation. This is important because it allows the prospect to meet the people who will actually work on his account. I also tried not to be there during those presentations but, instead, met the prospect afterwards, over a gin and tonic, when he was relaxed and seeking to get to know personalities in the agency.

Watch the trap

I do *not* believe the myth that any one man can turn a so-called 'non-creative' agency into a 'creative' agency; indeed I don't believe it has ever been done (although I have seen a number of highly creative agencies end up after a number of years producing very mediocre work). And I would advise creative people that if any agency offers you a creative director's chair on the premise 'Make us a hot-shop', he should turn it down. The existing clients don't want a hot-shop, and the existing agency hierarchy doesn't want a hot-shop. Believe me, any account person who does want to work for a more creative agency should not have a great deal of difficulty moving into one.

If I have made the creative director's job seem difficult, then that it because it *is* difficult. If I have made it seem impossible, let me correct the impression, since there are a good many creative directors today doing a very good job. The post is demanding, even challenging, and every creative person worth his salt should grab the opportunity to take it if it is ever offered. For as a colleague of mine (also a creative director) once so appositely said: 'It's the most fun you can have with your clothes on'.

Chapter 3

GOOD HABITS TO GET INTO

When I was a creative director, I used to make a point, once a day, of 'doing the rounds', i.e. calling on the people in my department and spending a few minutes chatting with them. There were several reasons for this. First, I could see who was busy, what they were working on, and how the ads were progressing. If the people in one office weren't busy then I could ask them about the workload, what ads were going through the system, and whether they would favour taking on another job, or whether it was just one of the natural lulls that happen in the best-run businesses. It was also an opportunity to check up in case any group had too much work, and see if they could use a little help so everything would be done on time. And, naturally, I was there to pick up the grouses; such-and-such an ad hadn't been accepted, such-and-such an account person was proving difficult over a certain point; somebody wanted advice on which director to use to make a TV commercial; somebody else just wasn't happy that day. At the same time as smoothing things over, I could pass on any good news. Perhaps the agency was in the offing for a new account; perhaps one of the other groups had held a very good meeting with a client.

19

Worry is the root of all evil

But sometimes, when I visited a team, they would be wrapped
in thought; worse, they might be surrounded by a haze of
anxiety because they were being pressed by copy dates to
find a solution to a certain problem, and they hadn't a clue
where it was going to come from. Ninety-nine times out of a
hundred, this was simply because they hadn't prepared themselves properly for the job. It has got to be understood that
effective, hard-working advertisements do not arrive out of
thin air. Copywriting is not a case of saying simply: 'OK lads,
let's think of a good idea'. Picking thoughts from the wide
blue yonder and attaching them to products may be what
the student or trainee thinks a creative person's job is. I have
even found some account people – and not inexperienced
ones either – who believe that is how things are done.

Begin at the start

It is nothing of the sort. Over the years I have learned there
is a lot to do before you finally settle down to make an ad.
You should be quite clear of the size of the advertisement
required: page, single-column ad, 48-sheet posters, two-
minute film or whatever. If you are doing a press ad then
you should rule out the type area on your layout pad so
you can see quite clearly how many square inches you have
to fill. Once you can *see* that space, get copies of the magazine
or newspaper in which the ad is to appear. Either find some
back numbers from your library or, if they have none, go out
to the bookstalls and buy the current issue.
   Read that magazine. Check the editorial for matters of
interest; get a sense of the style; see how technical the writing
is; note the kind of illustrations used, how they are captioned,
and whether there is a predominance of photographs or line
drawings. Check on the quality of the paper and find out how
the publication is printed (this will guide you as to how big
photographic illustrations must be to reproduce clearly) and
make a note in your head of any special techniques the
editor is using to increase readership. Then turn to the

recruitment pages: this will show you what kind of people read the magazine, what kind of jobs they do, what qualifications they have and how much money they earn. You see, already you are getting to know quite a bit about the audience you will be talking to. You can decide how technical your own writing must be, and whether to be subtle or straightforward in your approach.

Next, find out on what date your advertisement will appear, and whether that date has any special significance. It might be a jubilee for a certain manufacturer; it might be on a day when the publication is running a special supplement; or when a trade exhibition is about to be opened.

Look at the ad requisition to see if you are given colour or black and white to work in. If black and white, will colour (maybe just 'spot' colour — a single second colour) help to get your message over any better, and if so, how much extra will it cost? Where in the publication is your ad to run: inside front cover, next to the contents page, next to editorial, next to recruitment ads, inside back cover, outside back cover or run-of-paper (that is, wherever the make-up man on the publication feels like putting it).

Bleeding in the gutter

If you have a double-page spread, see whether you have the centre of the magazine to work with, then you don't have to worry about things like where your headline splits, or whether part of your picture will disappear in the gutter (the fold where the publication is stitched). Enquire whether your ad will bleed — that is be trimmed flush to the edge of the page (this normally costs about 10 per cent extra) or whether you are working to a type area, in which case your ad will have a white border round it. If you haven't got bleed, you might want to try and get it, since it will let you say more — I mean in terms of the forcefulness of your communication rather than in terms of content — bleed doesn't mean you should use more words.

Finally, check whether the publication has a correspondence section. This will give you an insight into what readers think, how literate they are, and what particular matters are currently on their minds. It may be that you can incorporate a particular subject into your ad (provided the insertion date if not so far ahead that readers will have forgotten the correspondence). A glance at the leader — most magazines have one — can also help. And keep an eye peeled on views which appear to be unpopular; it's worth knowing what not to say, as well as what people want to hear.

Right, the first part of your preparation is over. And you see how helpful it has been. Yet when I did my rounds I frequently found cases where the creative group not only didn't have a copy of the magazine their ad was to run in, they'd never even heard of it.

So you have the publication, you have drawn up the space in that publication you want to fill, you know when the ad is to run, now turn to the product.

You cannot find out too much about your product

If it is small enough to get onto your desk, put it there. If it's too big for that, get as many photographs of it as you can. And start to study. If you are writing a campaign for the product for the first time, and you have plenty of time, don't be afraid to ask to go round the factory. Few things can help you understand your client, and get the inside facts on how his goods are made, better than a tour of his works. Let me give you an example. I was once asked to write a campaign for Church Shoes. The simple fact was, they cost more wholesale than a great many shoes from other makers cost retail. So you see, we had a price problem. I wanted to find out where all the money was going.

I spent a day watching the shoes being made. The soles were stamped out of 2-inch-thick leather. They were stitched to the uppers with thread that was waxed by hand. The shoes were actually made in *pairs:* there was none of the business of making half a million left shoes, the same number of right shoes, and pairing them off at the end of the line. It took over 200 different operations to make a single shoe; each was polished by hand with camel hair brushes to give a scratch-free

22

shine; and the final embossing, with the size, style and brand name, was done in 22-carat gold. I came away convinced that although the shoes were very expensive, they were worth every penny.

I wouldn't have discovered any of this if I hadn't asked to go round the factory; and when the ad was written and presented to Church's managing director, even he didn't know everything about his shoes that my advertisement told him.

Information sells

And that is the next secret of making good ads. *Tell the reader something he doesn't know.* Now obviously you're not going to be able to do that if you simply write from your own general knowledge. So if you are going to advertise a car, you have first got to drive it; a food and you have first got to eat it; a refrigerator and you've got to go to a showroom and persuade an assistant to 'sell' it to you, while you compare it with the competition you are up against; a service — say car hire — and you have got to experience it; a job, and you've got to speak to the people who do it, find why they enjoy it, and how they got into it in the first place. First-hand experience of whatever you have to sell makes for first-rate ads. If you haven't got the straw, you can't make the bricks to build a sales argument. Once you've steeped yourself in the product and heard the story from the maker's point of view, find out what other people think about it. If you're selling a car, read the motoring correspondents; if you're selling a detergent, speak to the housewife; a beauty product, speak to the lady who uses it and find out why, and what it does for her. An independent, unbiased opinion is worth half-a-dozen claims from the maker, and that opinion is even more valuable if it comes from someone well qualified to comment. And don't forget the guard book. You may well discover, buried in the body text of an old ad, a fact with which to build a new headline. Now let me give you an example of how someone uncommitted to a brand can still help you sell it.

What about the workers?

I was asked to make an ad for a cooker. I went to see it being built and to the retailers to see how well it stood up surrounded by other cookers. Then I found a steel technician who hadn't made a cooker in his life but understood all about the gauge and quality of metals. I looked up an electrician who'd never wired a cooker but knew good work when he saw it. I spoke to an enameller who had worked on baths but not cookers, and finally chatted to an insulation expert (again, he had nothing to do with cookers but understood the insulation principles involved). All of them, when they saw the cooker for the first time, agreed it was good. Hence an ad that was headlined: A testimonial for Brand X cookers from four people who've never used one in their lives.

There is another reason why you should be completely *au fait* with your product. Not only will you make good ads, but you will be in an excellent position to explain and defend your work. An account person can destroy your ad if he comes up with a fact that you know nothing about. Not only will you look a fool, you will have proved to him that you simply haven't done your homework. On the other hand, few things impress a client more than the creative person who demonstrates he knows as much about the product as the man who actually manufacturers it. Demonstrating that you have researched it, checked up on how the public see it and dug out information for yourself immediately increases the client's confidence in you, and dismisses any suspicion that you are working from ignorance. He warms to your professionalism and is more inclined to accept your recommendations.

So now you know a lot about the magazine your ad is to appear in, a little about the people who read the magazine, and hopefully everything there is to know about the product you are selling. Now you have to find out about the people you are selling to. *Who is the customer?* To find out about the market, you can first go through all the documents likely to be in the agency. What age is the prospect? What does he earn? Where does he live? Where, and how does he buy? In

short, *who are you talking to?* I am going to say a lot more
about what we call in advertising jargon 'the target audience'
in Chapter 4, but you will get a tremendous amount of help
when you get down to making your ad if you can 'see' that
audience in your mind's eye.

You're part of a team, good buddy

Finally, you settle down to work. Be sure to remember, as
I said in Chapter 1, to work *with* your art director. I once
knew a writer who came into the agency early, before his art
director arrived, sat at his typewriter and freewheeled for an
hour, hoping an idea would come to life. This, in my view, is
quite the wrong way to work. Until you have thought of the
concept, until you have reached the main idea, you should
work on your layout pad. You might find it helps to actually
write headlines into the exact space that you have to fill
(remember I said to draw that out first). But before you
write anything, talk. Decide what your main thought should
be; use your colleagues' brains, because two heads can
produce more together than each can produce separately.
And remember, although you are the writer, there is no
reason why your art director can't come up with a headline:
or, for that matter, why you can't have the idea for the
picture. Get the feel of the man you are working with and
work as a team. I once knew a young copywriter who
couldn't bear his art director to write headlines. No matter
how good a headline appeared, if it came from the artist
this particular young man would say, 'Yes, very good', then
pause for a moment and try to paraphrase the same thought.
I'm not knocking persistence, or the attempt to refine and
express in fewer, better words a particular product claim,
I'm knocking the inability to acknowledge that an art
director can think of the right words. The problem arose
from a feeling of insecurity, and a need for that writer to
constantly prove himself. Happily, as he gained experience
and got closer to his art man, so he relaxed, and the two
became a very good team. Later they left that particular
agency for a nice, fat salary elsewhere. Of course, the problem

can apply in reverse to art directors, so if either of you find yourselves doing it to the other, stop.

A great idea, as David Bernstein says in his book *Creative Advertising* (Longmans), doesn't care who has it. And what matters is not who has it, but whether the other guy is big enough to recognise it. Or brave enough to say: 'That's rubbish' when a second-rate idea appears. Some of the art directors I've worked with were valuable because they could *discriminate* — the good from the bad, the better from the good — and they could put their finger on the best idea no matter where it came from (even from a media or account person).

'I' didn't do it, 'we' did it

Present your work as a team. When you agree what you are going to do, do it with a united front. You don't have to make it plain to the creative director that it was your idea, or that it was Charlie's idea; if he's a good creative director, he'll assume you worked together and not need to know where the initial spark came from. Sooner or later the true source of an idea makes itself felt: like murder it speaks with most miraculous organ.

There is another aspect of this relationship with your art director. There will be times when your colleague simply can't have an idea. This might go on for a time; try as he may, nothing he suggests comes up to his usual standard, and you find the onus of the work falling on you. Whatever you do, don't criticise him. For two reasons. One, because silent criticism doesn't just hurt the person it is directed at — *it inhibits him from returning to good form.* And two, if you silently nail him when he has a barren spell, then you'll be nailed yourself when you have one, and nothing is more destructive for either of you. This is not to say you should forever carry a deadweight. That is a waste of time and, eventually, if you keep providing the solutions, the other guy stops thinking for himself; his advertising brain seizes up.

I have worked with most types of art directors and one

thing is sure: the system that used to prevail in the old days, of the copywriter sitting in one room writing the words, then the mail-boy carrying them to another room where the art director added a picture, was a waste of the talent of both men. When we get on to how ads are made in more detail, I hope you will understand that the picture and the headline should work in conjunction with each other, and there can be times when neither makes sense on its own. More often than not, when that happens, you have made a very good ad, and it could never happen if the two men in the team didn't speak to each other.

A line and an outline

The method of working should be simple. You both kick around ideas for as long as you need, and then maybe put down two or three on a layout pad. They should consist only of a sketch of the illustration and a headline, and the message of the ad should come across as though you are making a poster. As you turn out the first draft ideas, pin them on your wall. Some groups like to give their ads what they call 'the overnight test', that is, they make no decision about them until the next day, when they can come into the office fresh and see if what seemed quite brilliant yesterday, still has the same impact 24 hours later. If it doesn't you should have no compunction about scrapping it. I once saw a 'house' ad for a particular agency which claimed that most places would present to their clients work this agency threw away.

When you are doing very small ads (by which I mean 2-, 4-, or 6-inch single or double columns), it can help to work *in that size space* on your layout pad. That way you get a true idea of how big the headline is going to appear and it's easy to tell how many words you can sensibly include. It may seem hard to start with, but since you have to take a long time to get things right (both looking right, and reading right), you pay much more attention to economy in words and speed of communication. You may not work like that later in your job-life, but when you are gaining experience and can't tell by instinct when your copy is overlength, it is a good habit to cultivate. The habit of drawing up the type area can help whatever size of ad you are doing. It can show you whether you need all the space to tell the story, or conversely whether you can't possibly tell the story in so small a space. Don't work directly onto your typewriter before you have a format worked out. The time to start tapping the keys is when you get down to making the body copy, and a good rule to remember here is that you should never use two words when one will do.

Poetry don't sell

Many copywriters, when they start off, take a great deal of time developing a style. What is much more important is that you get the *content* of the ad right. Alliteration, flowing phrases, puns, pretty turns of phrase may have their place, but it is way behind making sense of what you are saying, and communicating the message simply, clearly and concisely.

I once had a man come to me for an opinion on a piece of copy. I read it a couple of times, then sat down and together we condensed it into a third of its length without leaving out a single piece of relevant information. I thought the man would have been well pleased, but when I saw the ad type-set a few days later, it was back to its original length. And when I asked him about it, he said he wanted to preserve his style. This is sheer self-indulgence, since the best style to have is the most economic style. Readers don't have time (nor any inclination) to admire the style in which ads are composed. They want to know 'what's in it for me?'. So use short words, pithy words, and be as brief as you can, without missing out any point that will help make the sale. Remember, though you may aspire to being a poet, while you are being paid by a client you are a salesman, and a very business-like one too. Interesting copy is copy that moves at a pace, gives a real reward for reading and keeps telling you things you didn't know and yet can easily believe. There is a great deal of value in a piece of advertising copy that *astonishes,* provided always that it rings true.

So, to summarise

First use the tools at your command: pen and layout pad. Get down the size of the ad you have to make. Then get the publication in which it is to appear. Then find out everything you can about the product (if possible keep it on your desk). Then find out all you can about the person you want to sell it to. Then start thinking. Talk over your thoughts with your art director and put two or three of them down on paper. Pin the paper to your wall and give it 'the overnight test'. Be ruthless with anything that is less than excellent. Economise with your words. Try to create telegrams — that is pictures and headlines that telegram the message. Make allowances for each other, and recognise that neither of you has a monopoly of the words or the pictures. In the end, together, you should have made one good ad, which, as they say, is what it's all about.

Chapter 4

THERE ARE ONLY TWO KINDS OF ADVERTISING

There are:

Newspaper and magazine ads
Television ads
Cinema ads
Direct mail ads
Mail order ads
Retail ads
Financial ads
Recruitment ads
Classified ads
Prestige ads
Legal ads
Book and record club ads
Health insurance ads
Posters

And you can probably think of more. So what do I mean when I say there are only two kinds of ads? Simple; whatever kind of ad you pick from the above list, it must fall into one of two categories:
1   Ads where there is something to say.
2   Ads where there is nothing to say.

Let us deal with the first obvious objection to that paragraph, which is, as any experienced creative person will tell you, that every ad should have something to say. Very true. And it is the creative person's job to make sure every ad says something. But there are many occasions when there is little or nothing of substance to say. For example, you are asked to make a commercial for a tin of beans. Now what can you tell the million or so housewives who buy them every day about a tin of beans? Isn't anything you say about them likely to be such common knowledge that your commercial ends up being utterly banal? There is, in fact, virtually nothing you can tell a woman about baked beans that *(a)* will interest her and *(b)* she doesn't already know. That's what I mean by the kind of advertising where the creative person has nothing to say.

But first let us look at the area where there is something to say. Happily there are a great number of products which carry good stories and allow creative people to devise factual claims and produce informative advertising. To name a few, I would say ads for cars, washing machines, Hi Fi, insurance, holidays and any kind of entertainment, all have plenty to say. And in those cases (and obviously I have only listed a minute fraction of them) the important thing is — *say it*.

First silver rule

That is the first principle in making good ads: *when you have something to say, say it.* But having made such a positive statement, I want to make a further point. You may have a product about which there is a great deal to say. In that case you must simplify your story, so you spearhead your ad, whether it be a press ad or a commercial, with a single thought. It should be the essence of the claim you want to make, the one aspect of the product you most want people to remember. You will make very little headway if you try to produce work that has a great many ideas bursting out of it; in a 30-second TV commercial your audience will not be able to remember more than one thought. When you make a press ad, your headline and picture are unlikely to be able to

31

communicate more than one thought. And in the cases where you have a complex story to tell, you may need to spend a lot of time discussing with the client, the account people and your creative partner what the one thought should be.

Let me quote an example. A tyre manufacturer I once worked with invented a new tyre. It was a radial tyre. It had a completely new tread design. Under the rubber was a nylon strip which reduced wear. Underneath the nylon strip was a steel belt, which pushed the tyre down firmly on the road and greatly increased grip in wet weather. And the tyre was being offered at a very competitive price. You can see at once there is a great deal to say about such a product, but what is most important is that any advertising communicates one major thought. The supporting sales points can be mentioned, of course, but one big idea should come out of any campaign devised for that tyre. The thought we finally chose was SAFETY — that this new tyre increased the safety of motorists, whatever the weather conditions. The commercials concentrated on situations where a driver needed his tyre to grip the road. We featured a windscreen shattering on a motorway, where the car came to a swift, safe halt; a Y junction where a cyclist swerved in front of the car, which was able to stop in time; and a demonstration of some tailor's dummies falling in front of the car, which was able to avoid crushing them (the parallel with real people is obvious). The point I want to emphasise is that all the ads were single-minded. They had something to say — that the tyre made driving safer — and they said it simply, yet very dramatically, time and again. There was no question of dissipating the advertising effort by making one film about the steel, one about the nylon, one about the low price, and so on. So to summarise so far, if you have something to say, say it. Say it simply, say it dramatically, and be completely single-minded about your claim. To quote an old advertising adage, repetition is reputation.

The unique proposition

One advertising man took this principle to a very firm

conclusion. Mr Rosser Reeves, who was first a copywriter, then creative director, and finally a senior partner in a leading American agency, developed what he called the philosophy of the Unique Selling Proposition. This is abbreviated now to USP. Reeves' idea was simple; the agency had to go through the benefits of the product until they could find something unique to say about it.

Or, if there really was nothing unique, then they had to find a feature of the product which nobody else was using and make it their own. This unique feature was the Unique Selling Proposition and was meant to represent the one feature which that product, and only that product, could offer the consumer. Reeves attached this philosophy to the agency he worked at (Ted Bates and Co.) so it too had a USP. He helped to build it into one of America's largest and most successful shops. When Ted Bates bought their way into British advertising they brought the USP philosophy with them, and it led to some very strange campaigns. When advertising a chocolate button with a sugar glazing, the USP they found was: 'melts in your mouth, not in your hand'. And for a boiled sugar sweet: 'double-wrapped to keep in the freshness'. Never mind what the sweets tasted like, or that sweets make kids happy so the commercials should be happy. Bates were determined to find USPs, even if they were so far down the line of customer requirements as to be virtually irrelevant. It took them some years, and the departure of not a few creative people, to accept that there were times when a product simply did not have a viable Unique Selling Proposition. But it is not my intention to knock the idea of USP; I use it to emphasise the importance of being single-minded in your advertising, looking for the main sales point, and then pushing it home in all the promotional material so you make a real impact.

Second silver rule

So much for those times when the product offers you something to say. Now what about when you have nothing to say? I include in this product category beers, petrols and oils, steam-baked breads, tinned fruits, most cigarettes, butter, margarines, and most shampoos, deodorants and hair sprays. Not only is there very rarely anything you can say about them the public doesn't already know, they are also products which command the largest appropriations. They spend a great deal of money, they often use a great many changes of copy, and yet there is nothing to say. The principle here is quite simple; *when you have nothing to say, use showmanship*.

As usual, an example will help to clarify. Campbells soup is very big in America and the company spend a lot of money on TV. But since almost every American has enjoyed Campbells soup at some time, and the soups rarely change, there is little or nothing you can say that the customer doesn't already know. Campbells devised one commercial that started in a kitchen, with a woman opening the can, but suddenly we are in the middle of a terrific Busby Berkley routine, with hundreds of pretty girls singing and dancing, and the centre-point of the stage is a giant Campbells can. The set is astonishing, the dancing amazing, the spectacle is breath-taking (and it obviously cost a great deal of money); and the excuse for it all is in the last line when we come back to the kitchen scene and the woman's husband says something like: 'Marj, why do you have to make such a performance of everything?'. Sure, it's corny, but it doesn't matter; what matters is that the audience has been glued to their sets for 60 seconds watching a piece of terrific entertainment, at the centre of which is a giant can of Campbells soup. The product is on the screen for 90 per cent of the showing time, yet no one is bored, no one switches off, they are having the Campbell name burned into their memory and being royally entertained at the same time. You see the idea; when you have nothing to say, use showmanship.

Another brief summary, so you have got the two most important principles about making ads fixed firmly into your mind. First, when you have something to say, say it. Secondly, when you have nothing to say, use showmanship. If you remember these principles, you will save yourself hours of heartache searching for stories to tell about products that have no stories to tell. At the same time you will avoid foolish campaigns, where there is a real story but you bury it under a welter of borrowed interest.

Don't seek where you won't find

In my early days as a copywriter, the idea that I might be presented with a product that had a quarter of a million pounds to spend, and about which there would be virtually nothing to say, never occurred to me. And this 'blindness' to the way campaigns were written led to some sleepless nights, as I turned over in my mind the problems of writing a campaign about, say, lager, which had a certain taste (but no very distinctive one), was brewed for a brief spell, then distributed. With those few meagre facts, how could I ever produce an exciting advertising campaign? If only someone had pointed out to me that it was no use looking for an advertising campaign which talked exclusively about the product.

So how is it done? Let us consider a highly successful campaign for lager — the one for Heineken. Once it's pointed out, it is easy to see that the advertising is not about the lager *per se,* it's about the effect a beer might have if it could reach the parts of the body that beer cannot reach. I am in no way decrying the advertising (I consider it brilliant), but I am showing the would-be copywriter that if he directs his attention solely to the product, he may never find good creative solutions. The answer lies, as I have already said, in showmanship: show policemen wriggling their toes as the lager revives them; show a potter using his skill again as the lager takes effect. It's highly imaginative stuff, and it captures the imagination of drinkers all over the country, but no way is it about Heineken. It's an illogical extention of the effect good drink has on the psyche.

Animal imagery

Another product I listed amongst those that have nothing to say is petrol. Let us look at what was probably the most effective campaign of the nineteen-sixties: the job done for Esso — 'Put a tiger in your tank'. Figures show that this campaign persuaded more drivers to switch from their usual petrol to Esso, than any other gasoline campaign before or since. But is the campaign about the petrol? Certainly not, it's about getting the power of a tiger into your engine; the decorations round the pump hose-pipes, the tiny tiger tails to fix to your driving mirror and the majestic tigers leaping over the hoardings have nothing to do with the petrol. All you can tell drivers about the real Esso is that it comes in a number of grades, is refined to suit any engine, and you can pick it up anywhere in the country, all of which they know perfectly well already. You see, now it is pointed out, that the ads didn't talk about Esso Petrol at all, and if they had they would have been very dull ads. But hit on a slogan like 'Put a tiger in your tank' and you have a theme you can develop for years. Forget the technical details; go for excitement, fun, and the ingeniousness of an idea. And offer those humorous little give-aways like tiger tails and you'll have crowds queueing at the pumps.

There is another petrol campaign that worked well at the pumps — the Shell Make Money campaign. This was a contest where you picked up half a fake bank note every time you bought petrol, and if you were lucky, you got two halves that fitted together perfectly, which you could exchange for hard cash. The technique was eventually declared illegal, but that is not the point here; the point is that it wasn't about Shell Petrol — it was about collecting enough half notes to make money.

Have gamez with beanz

Let us consider one final example. I started this chapter by telling you there was nothing to say about cans of baked beans; yet Heinz spend up to a million a year advertising them, and they do it very effectively. But do they talk about the beans? Not directly, no. In one campaign they show young children saying witty rhymes about where they had tea and what they had to eat. The kids are the main attraction, and

the fun in the rhymes makes us listen and grin. But they
don't tell you how many beans are in the can, nor what the
beans are (who knows what baked beans are?) nor how the
delicious tomato sauce if made; the only fact you can gather
from the Heinz baked beans advertising is that a million
housewives open up a tin every day. This in itself is
impressive, and they add that brilliant slogan Beanz Meanz
Heinz at the end. The ads are not about beans, they are about
the people who buy them, and about the fun you can have if
you play games with the letter z.

Look beyond the product

Those examples should show the young copywriter that he
has to look further than the product if he is going to develop a
campaign the advertiser can put money behind. He can talk
about who uses the product, where they use it, when and how
they use it, or why they use it. These techniques I will deal
with much more fully later in this book. I have spent so much
time developing this theme to help you avoid the pitfalls I
stumbled into in my career. I made a point in the last
chapter of telling you to put the product on your desk
before you started to write about it, but you could spend a
year staring at a can of beans and not get a campaign out of
it that was worth a row of beans. This is why it is vital that
you go for facts; discover the story of the baked bean, where
it comes from, how it's grown, who first imported it. Do
anything to get information, because without it you will
never get an idea. But in the last analysis, with products of
this kind, it is showmanship that counts. And this is where
the writer and art directors have to put on their caps and
think. But even wild thinking is not enough unless you know
the techniques you can use to help you devise campaigns.
There are a lot of them, and as you progress in the business
you will learn to recognise when a particular technique has
been used. Chapters 6, 7 and 8 list many techniques you will
find useful. If you are an ingenious writer, you may, as
you gain experience, invent some of your own; and you
can be sure, if you do, that the rest of the business will be

hard on your heels, taking your idea and using it for themselves, with their own particular twist added to make it just that little bit different. There's nothing new under the sun, but there are certainly new ways of seeing and solving old problems and that is part of our craft.

Easy campaigns — and hard ones

I would like to end this chapter with a word about campaigns that strike you as brilliant; you must learn to judge whether they rest on the ingeniousness of the writer and art director *finding* something to say; or whether the interest was actually in the product itself, and all they did (all?) was dig it out. You may have noticed some ads, for contraception, for road safety and for moderation in drinking for example, have received acclaim from advertising people, and rightly so. But it has to be said — and this is no denigration of the skill of the creative people involved — that contraception *is* a subject that arouses a great deal of interest, not to say controversy. And road safety allows creative people to show road accidents — and how they actually happen — which, in itself, is mighty interesting. And the very clever techniques of the anti-booze advertising campaigns, which invite you to find out for yourself whether you are on the path to alcoholism, are fascinating to read because they can ring a bell in our daily lives. Please be clear, I an not decrying the skills of the writers who made these campaigns; less talented people would have made a much worse job of them. I *am* saying that some subjects are intrinsically interesting, and I think you will find it easier to do good work on these subjects than you will on products which, of themselves, have little or nothing to make you sit up and think.

So, one final summary. Decide whether your product has anything to say; if it has, say it. If it hasn't, don't waste fruitless hours trying to dig out some obscure fact which you hope will give you a campaign. Use showmanship. Look well outside the product itself to the people, the times, the places and the ways the product is used. Above all, be interesting. The next chapters will show you how.

Chapter 5

WORK ON WHAT TO SAY, NOT ON HOW TO SAY IT

One of the hardest things to learn when you first begin to
write copy is how *not* to do it. This is because the average
Joe thinks the craft consists mainly of being clever with
words. That's not what copywriting is about at all. Someone
else said a copy person was an advocate for a client's product
and it was his job to make out the best possible case for it;
I define it simply as 'making someone want to do something'.
You make them want to own a particular car, or use a
particular service, or wear particular clothes. And while you
should be able to use words cleverly, it is much more
important that you are *articulate* in print than that you can
play the fool with grammar, spelling or quotations. Throw
away your Thesaurus, put down your books of *bon mots,* and
jettison all that junk of half-remembered phrases from your
poetry and English literature classes. None of that is going
to help you, and the only reference book any copywriter
really needs is a dictionary, and that only because he may
need to correct his spelling.

There is another attitude of mind that inhibits people
from making good ads, and that is the need to impress. This
is very invidious, and I am not suggesting there's anything

wrong with the writer wanting himself and his work to be well thought of. But you can end up in a situation where you sit down with your art director, and each says to the other: 'This ad has got to be great!'. And the very desire to make a 'great' ad actually impedes you doing it, because you are starting at the wrong end.

There is nothing out of place with imposing high creative standards on your work; in fact I believe the creative team should be its own toughest critic. But do not work to make impressive ads; work to sell the product or service and you will impress if the ad does the job that it's intended to. The way to start work is to prepare yourself as I described in Chapter 3. You get your layout pad, your felt-tip pens, the paper your ad is going into and the product (hopefully) on your desk. Then refer to 'The Strategy'.

The advertising strategy

An advertising strategy is prepared by the client, account people and creative people, together. They examine all the aspects of the product, the market, distribution, profit target, and the appropriation backing the product, then devise a plan of campaign. When the plan is agreed the agency sets it down in a document and sends it to the client. The client passes it round the people in his company who want to know what direction the advertising is to take. Those people may make comments which the client will then relay back to the agency. If corrections are required, the agency will make them, the account and creative people working together again. The revised version is returned to the client and he seeks agreement to it from the people at his end. Finally it comes back to the agency signed and sealed, and the agency then sets out a strategy document, which should be the bible on how the product is to be promoted.

A strategy will tell you:
Who the target audience is.
What offer you have to put to them.
What evidence you have to show the offer is worthwhile.
What final impression you want to leave.

That may not be the way the strategies read in your office, since every agency has its own method of putting down what the advertising should achieve, but that should be the gist of what they mean. Forms may differ, but the content should be the same. Let there be no mistake about how important a strategy is. Nor should anyone feel it is a device to restrict the creative person. A strategy is the result of hard thinking by everyone concerned with the product. Creative people should always be consulted before the strategy is drawn up, and any account person who dares to produce a strategy without consulting the creative department deserves all the flack he gets.

Strategies help you sell your work

You, as a creative person, should be grateful for a strategy for a number of reasons. First, it points you in a direction and puts you under a discipline that can prevent hours of useless work. A strategy shouldn't tell you exactly what to do in your ad; it can be more helpful in telling you what not to do. Dozens of irrelevant ideas which you might have been tempted to develop can be discarded thanks to the strategy. It saves you time, it saves you work, it stops you going up creative blind alleys. If you like, it's a map that tells you where the gold is buried and says 'Dig here'. Another fact to remember is that strategies protect your work; they make it much more difficult for a client to reject a campaign for the wrong reasons. If your ads talk to the audience defined in the strategy, if each makes a promise as defined in the strategy and does it in an interesting and out-of-the-ordinary manner, then the work cannot easily be rejected. Irrational judgements, subjective views, whether or not the client likes the colour of the model's dress and so on, are of no weight when checking to see if a campaign is a true interpretation of a strategy.

And if the client's people believe the strategy is right, and the agency people agree (because they all drew it up together), and if it can be shown that each ad is 'on strategy' then there is no reason not to accept the campaign. So you see, far from being an enemy to creativity, a strategy can be the creative man's best friend.

First important question

So, there you are with your layout pad, your pens and the product; you pick up the strategy and ask yourself: *who are we talking to?* In my view, this is one of the two most important questions you will ever have to ask as a creative person. The strategy answers it by defining the target audience. And you may find it written something like: 'AB mothers between ages 25 and 45'. I want to emphasise that although this is the target audience (to use professional jargon) it is not who you are talking to, it is a *category* of person. What's the difference? Well, young to middle-aged women, with one or more children and husbands who earn between £5,000 and £25,000 a year, are a large spectrum of the population and you cannot write ads to a spectrum.

Very often you will have a product that will appeal to millions; it's almost certain that the media you buy will reach millions; but when you get down to making your ad, you have got to be much more specific. You have to decide which of the families in that range of incomes (£5,000 to £25,000 remember) you think you are most likely to influence. Since you are talking to mothers, what effect will children have on whether they buy or not? Can you see, in your mind's eye, the type of woman who is most likely to be influenced by your ad? Can you hear how she talks? Can you devise an approach to your product that will make her listen? Is it possible that you have met one or two women who might buy the product? Could you name one of them? It it Mrs Jones who lives just a couple of doors away? You're sure? Then *that's who you're talking to.*

Talk sense

Now you wouldn't talk to Mrs Jones as though she were a fool would you? You wouldn't say anything to her in print, the sense of which you would blush to say to her face. In fact you would try to reason with her and show her good argument as to why she should buy the product you have to sell. And because you know Mrs Jones, and how she thinks, you are in a much better position to know how to talk to her. You will speak sensibly, intelligently, with a smile here, a sound selling point there, all the time keeping her attention and making her feel pleased that you think she is worth all this time and trouble. Because you 'see' Mrs Jones when you write the ad, and not just a category of person, you are much more direct, much more personal, much closer to the right tone of voice to use.

> *If every copywriter knew who he was talking to when he made an ad, and could 'see' that person as someone he had met, at once the quality of all advertisements would improve.*

Let's summarise what we have agreed in this chapter so far. First, copywriting is not just a matter of having games with words; you have to put down a sensible case for a product. You have to direct that case to a target audience, which is defined in the strategy. But you never write to a category of person; you narrow your audience down to someone you actually know. And then you talk to that person, making sure you use the right tone of voice and speak with the right amount of intelligence. And when you have produced the ad, you have got a strategy to help you defend it when you present it to clients. You see, suddenly the craft is coming clear; it's not just a matter of ideas from the wide blue yonder (as I've said before) it's a matter of logic, common-sense and sound thinking.

Second important question

Good, you now know who you are talking to, which I repeat is one of the two most important questions you must ask. The second question, equally important, is *what do you want to say?* And again we turn to the strategy, where point two says: 'What is the offer you want to make?'.

You remember the example we used of the tyre with a great number of sales points? And how we narrowed them down to one main thought, SAFETY? Well a strategy should do just that for you: narrow down the main thought. Which brings me to the title of this chapter: *work on what to say.* And only after you are utterly certain of that should you concern yourself with how to say it. The style, the actual choice of words, the rhythm of your sentence, the pun if there is one, or the twist you are trying to work on a well known phrase or saying, all that is a matter of style, or form, or *how* to say a thing. It is important, but only after you are totally clear on *what* you want to say. Because there is one thing utterly certain about making good ads:

> *You will never write an effective headline unless you find something effective to say.*

The effect can be enhanced by the form of the words; the impression you create can be more forceful; you can get a promise remembered for longer. But no one will remember anything at all, unless *what* you say is memorable.

If it sounds stupid when you say it, don't write it

Never be satisfied with a strategy unless it gives you something to say, and never write a headline, however literary, alliterative or poetic, that says nothing. Don't worry in the first place whether your words are slick, polished or trip off the tongue easily; ask yourself: what am I trying to say? Speak the promise out loud to the person you work with; that way you can tell if it makes sense, is part of the language of life and stands up as an offer. And you will be able to tell, if you say it to your colleague's face and have in mind the person you are talking to, whether it is likely to be believed. It might be helpful at this point to go step-by-step through a case history, where I can name a real product and we end up with a real campaign. Let us look at the advertising for Ryvita Crispbread. First, a little background to the product.

Ryvita had been sold for many years as a good-tasting crisp-bread. It cost very little to buy, and was highly popular; everyone knew what it tasted like and most people were happy with the taste. But sales had reached a plateau.

The agency discovered that at the time there was a tremendous boom in the slimming market; sales of products to help people lose weight were rising dramatically. A few questions to the makers of Ryvita, about the calorific content of the crispbread, confirmed that not a single crispbread on the market — even those claiming to be starch-reduced — had fewer calories than Ryvita. Here was a chance to enter a booming market and extend the uses of Ryvita, by offering it as a way not only to enjoy a good-tasting food, but as an aid to slimmers. The agency creative and account men got together to write a strategy:

Who is the target audience?
Women who want to slim.
What offer do we put to them?
Ryvita can help you slim.
What evidence is there that this is true?
No crispbread has fewer calories.
What final impression do we want to leave?
Ryvita really works.

Since this was a new business pitch, we didn't send the strategy to client to get his agreement (which you will recall is usual practice if the agency already holds the account). We decided we would sell the potential client our strategy when he came into the agency to meet us and see our presentation, and then demonstrate that the advertisements interpreted it accurately.

So the creative people got to work, and the first question, if you remember, is *who are we talking to?* The strategy defined it as women who want to slim; so, did I know anyone who wanted to slim? Yes — Miss X. I know she has a healthy scepticism of advertisements, but she really does want to slim, and I think I can work on ways to get her to listen to an argument.

What interests Miss X?

The most difficult problem is that she knows Ryvita of old and has never looked on it as a slimming aid. So I have to *change her attitude,* and get her thinking this good-tasting bread is also a great help in trimming her figure. What are good ways to talk to 20-year-old Miss X? I know she is interested in fashions; that's one of the reasons she want to slim. So I get some pictures of the very latest dresses from a leading London designer, and the models look really terrific, and I put a headline over each dress:

Like it? Ryvita will help you get into it.

This is a bit of a surprise, because I know Miss X has never considered Ryvita as a slimming bread; in fact she's probably never thought of Ryvita at all, apart from those times when she's munched a bit off the lunch table. So I have used the fashions to grab her attention but at the same time I am making a good promise, and the ad is on strategy. Also, if I want, I can go on for years showing different dresses on different models but keeping the same headline. I have, in fact, got a campaign. I decided to give the idea the 'overnight test'.

Fatness or fitness?

What else is Miss X interested in? Well, I know she believes one way she can lose weight is to do exercises; I've seen her wonder whether Yoga might help her figure; I know she's

---

THE INCH WAR

Making words collide is a good technique of saying something ordinary in an extraordinary way. The inch belt improves the headline. The pack is small because you don't need to tell people what a pack of Ryvita looks like. The copy starts with a fact. The baseline was subsequently changed from 'Ryvita wants you to win', to 'Ryvita helps you win'. (Art director: *Paul Arden)*

The Inch War

There are over two million Britons fighting the inch war.

If you want to be losing, Ryvita can help.

You need to eat fewer calories. No crispbread has fewer than Ryvita.

But you don't want to starve.

Ryvita helps you stave off that hungry feeling. You do want to enjoy your diet.

The crisp, natural, nutty whole rye taste

of Ryvita sees to that.

Now perhaps you see why Ryvita is the most eaten crispbread.

It makes the inch war less of a fight.

Ryvita helps you win

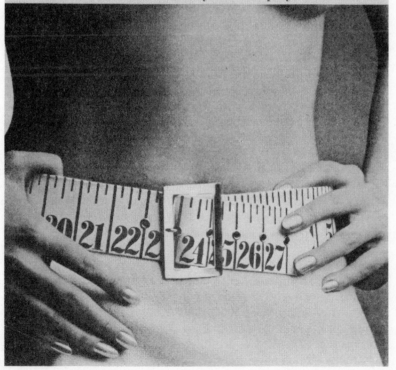

considered going to keep-fit classes (and so have millions
of women like her). So I get some shots of a slender and
pretty girl in a leotard, doing her exercises. And I put a headline over the upstretched arms:

Which slims best? Exercise or Ryvita?

Again this contains the element of surprise, and it's on
strategy, makes a promise, and has enough life in it, showing
different girls doing different exercises, to become a
campaign. The problem is, how do I answer the question
posed in the headline? I can't say Ryvita slims more than
exercises, because Miss X simply won't believe me. But
perhaps I can say that both Ryvita and exercises are equally
good at slimming. And provided I stress that Ryvita has to
be eaten as part of a calorie-controlled diet, and produce
examples of women who have actually lost weight with
Ryvita, there is nothing to stop this idea becoming a good
campaign. I decided to give this idea the 'overnight test'.

Now do you see how these ideas were arrived at because I
knew *who I was talking to,* and I knew *what I wanted to say.*
Is it clear that, once you have got an audience fixed in your
mind, creative solutions suggest themselves? You know what
pictures are interesting, you know what claims are believable,
you can judge the right tone of voice to use. And there is no
worry about polishing the words in the headlines. Since I
have decided *what* I want to say, it's easy to find the best,
least tricky way of saying it.

Those two campaigns stayed on our walls for several days,
but the question that kept coming back to me was: were they
surprising enough? Would they be strong enough to change
the current attitude to Ryvita, which was that it was a home-
spun good-tasting product? That was when I turned to
technique. (Techniques are fully dealt with in the next three
chapters.) Being absolutely certain *what to say,* I began to
work on *how to say it.* I know that one thing I can do to
build a good headline is make words collide. Which means
putting a few words together that have never been put together before. Spend a few days considering the problem, and
the brain can suddenly produce exactly the right phrase:

The Inch War. Ryvita wants you to win.

Now what I want you to take out of this case history is
not the fact that there are a number of ways to go to create
a campaign (which, of course, there are) but the order of
priorities. You must have a set way of working, or you will
end up in that terrible haze of anxiety which is so unhelpful
— wondering whether you should be in the business at all.
You must have a system, and the one that I have found gives
the best results is:
1   Agree on the strategy.
2   Decide who you are talking to (and remember that
    means pinpointing an actual person).
3   Decide what you want to say.
Only when all those things are absolutely clear in your
mind should you work on the form the words take, which is
why I have headed this chapter the way I have. When you
know all about the product, can picture who you are making
the ad for, and have honed down the product claim, then
you turn to technique and make the final two or three ads
to pin on your wall.

You can achieve greatness

I could go through several case histories, but the point about
working to a system is always the same. And even if I
describe *what* I did as closely as I can, what you really want
to know is *how* I did it. When all is said and done, the would-
be copy craftsman wants to know how to have an idea, and
often simply describing ideas that have been arrived at is of
no real help. It has been said that true creativity is something
you are born with, and that it cannot be taught; there
may be a grain of truth in that. But it is quite incorrect to say
that a young, inexperienced copywriter cannot be taught to
become a first-rate craftsman; of course he can, and indeed,
that is the aim of this book. What I would impress on you is
that there is no profit in worry, and you will never write the
best work you can do if you worry over it; learning to work
to a system helps prevent worry. Good copywriters can be

made; they are not simply born. I don't mean there aren't the odd one or two people in the business with a natural instinct for the work; of course there are. But most of us (and I include myself) have to be taught and you learn by *getting priorities straight*. In fact there are only two qualifications I would ask of the trainee writer: first, you must want to do the job; second, you must be willing to make sufficient effort to get results. If at first you don't succeed, you know what you have to do.

How you have an idea depends very much on what you do, which is why I have put so much stress on the practicalities of the job, and have not dwelt, as yet, on the need for any inspiration. Every moment spent finding facts about the product, about the market, about the customer, and about what you want to tell him, will pay dividends when you come to make your ad. Every fact can become a potential headline. Never try to speak to everyone; you will end up reaching no one. Dale Carnegie, who wrote *How to Make Friends and Influence People,* once said: 'Why should anyone be interested in you, unless you are first interested in them?'. If you want people to read, or listen to, and believe in your work, bear the question in mind.

Chapter 6

SOME TECHNIQUES

It will help you very much, when you are making your advertisement, if you know beforehand *how* it will be read. This matter has been the subject of much research, and the answers are quite specific. There is a definite route the eye takes over each ad. Let's say the reader is skimming through a newspaper or magazine, he turns the page and there is your work, full of promise, waiting to catch his attention: what happens?

First, his eye goes to the picture. Then he reads the headline. Then he moves down to the bottom right-hand corner of the advertisement, to see who is paying the bill. And, generally speaking, that is as far as most people get with most advertisements. As an aside here, it is worth mentioning that it has been estimated that in an average day, the average person has the opportunity to see between a 1000 and 1500 different sales messages. It seems a lot until you remember how many posters you pass, how many buses with ads on pass you, and how publicity is pouring out of radio stations, TV sets and the pages of newspapers and magazines all the time.

Cash down the drain

Of these 1500 or so advertisements, the researchers estimate that the average man or woman remembers between seven and ten. The figures vary, depending on the company that conducts the research, when it's done, and where, but if you reckon that out of every 1500 ads seen or heard, about ten make an impression, you won't be far out. These figures should give you pause for thought; it's obvious right away that a lot of advertisers are spending money and getting very little in return. It's also obvious how important it is to master the craft of ad-making, so that instead of doing work by so-called 'instinct', you use the techniques available to make sure your ads get into the top ten.

Right, let us suppose you have caught the customer's eye, he's scanned your picture, headline and logo, and is still interested in what you have to say. Where does he look next? If you are using a squared-up photograph as your illustration, and if you have set a caption under it — possibly in a small italic face as is used in a number of newspapers — the reader's eye will go to this caption next.

If you have still kept him interested, and if you have used cross-headings in your ad, or small drawings, charts or graphs, the eye will scan over these next, picking out the salient points of your argument. Finally, if you have kept his attention throughout this eye-journey, and he has been stimulated into wanting to know still more about what you have to sell, your reader will start on the body text proper.

That, according to the best research, is how people read advertisements. Now let us go back to the beginning and see what it can teach us about the craft of making ads.

HELP THE TWO OF US

Showing half of anything is a technique of making an ordinary picture look extraordinary. The headline means little or nothing without the picture. The copy was written only after visits to hospitals and talks with psychiatric nurses. (Art director: Ron Brown)

Help the two of us.

Becoming ill in the mind is not rare, nor frightening nor incurable.

One woman in six and one man in nine will go into hospital for mental treatment at some time in their lives.

Most recover and return to normal life.

But while they are unwell they need nurses to care for them.

Life as a psychiatric nurse means you work at helping people come to terms with themselves.

The job is immensely varied as you have to be friend, counsellor, listener, observer and know a little about occupational therapy and social work.

You have professional status, responsibility and can work both in the hospital, and in the community.

Both men and women are needed.

If nursing hurt minds sounds like a job you might do well, please post the coupon.

ABOUT THE PICTURE. The problem of being 'in two minds', and thus finding a decision impossible, is a common trait in some mental disorders. The picture is symbolic of this.

Nurse the mentally ill.
A job for understanding people.

Please send me more facts about psychiatric nursing.

Name (Mr/Miss/Mrs) _____

Address _____

_____

_____

Age _____

To: The Chief Nursing Officer, Dept. of Health and Social Security,
P.O. Box 702, London SW20 8SZ. (In Scotland, write to:–
The Chief Nursing Officer, St. Andrew's House, Edinburgh EH1 3DE.)

Use square pictures

People look at pictures before they read headlines. Surely
then, the more of the story the picture tells, the more you
will have communicated immediately. Later in this chapter I
will list the 12 subjects that most make people read; knowing
what they are will help you compose the kind of shots that
get most attention. Right now, it's worth remembering that
newspapers and magazines most often use squared-up
photographs. Since they are the kind of illustrations people
are used to seeing most, and since they also offer you the
best chance of good reproduction, you would be well advised
to use them whenever you can. Cut-outs are quite unusual,
so use them only when you have good reason.

The importance of headlines

The second stop on this eye-journey is the headline. As a
copywriter you should make no mistake: the headline is the
most important part of your advertisement. If it doesn't
communicate, your ad won't communicate, irrespective of
how powerful a picture you have used, or how tastefully
the layout has been done. I advise you to spend more time
working on your headline than any other of your words,
and to take great care over what that headline says. One
creative director I know says that any fool can write body
copy, but it takes a real craftsman to create compelling
headlines. (Certainly, if your headline is rejected, your ad is
almost invariably dead.
   One point I cannot emphasise too strongly. There can be
times when a headline does not need an illustration; but
there can *never* be a time when an illustration doesn't need
a headline. Of course you will see ads that go straight into
the body copy from the picture: I call these ads 'headless
wonders'. They are the occasions when the copywriter has
copped-out. Advice to art directors — never let your writer
make you run an ad without a headline. If he suggests it,
tell him not to be so damned lazy. A great picture deserves
a great line to back it up; even the painting of the Mona

Lisa in the Louvre needs a small brass plate underneath reading 'La Gioconda by Leonardo da Vinci'.

What makes headlines good?

First, they should always work *with* the picture. They should tell you one part of the story, while the picture tells the rest. Sometimes a headline can make no sense at all on its own. And a picture on its own can be a mystery (see page 53). When the two come together, however, the whole story is revealed, with punch and originality.

Never use a headline to repeat what the picture is saying. And never simply illustrate a headline. *Let the two parts do their own half of the work,* so when you see them as an entity the story comes across quick and clear, the way it should on a poster. Every good ad should be able to stand as a poster; the reader should never have to dip into the smallprint in order to understand the *nub* of the story.

Here is another fact research has discovered. The average reader spends about 1½ seconds on most advertisements. That's all the time you've got to shout: 'We've got something for you!'. And you must get the readers' attention in a manner that is *relevant* to your sales message. For example: you may want to write a headline: 'Bags of Gold Free!'. Now if the bags of gold *are* free, that's a good headline, but if you have to enter a competition to win them, or if they're only free if you go prospecting in the Rockies and dig the gold up yourself, then it's not a good headline. Any reader you have conned into the advertisement will feel very exasperated with you, and that irritation will be reflected onto the product you are trying to sell. As Leo Burnett once said: 'I can get attention by having a man come downstairs with a sock in his mouth. But it's a rotten ad unless that sock is totally relevant.'

Apply polish and buff hard

Style is important when you write headlines. Not as important as content — *what* you say — but not to be dismissed as not mattering at all. One good tip to remember when you are polishing a headline is to throw out the present participle. 'Watch sales *going* through the roof' can be trimmed to 'Watch sales *go* through the roof' with no loss of meaning or impact. Ninety-nine times out of a hundred the *ing* is unnecessary in headlines (or body copy for that matter). It's a good idea to write in the present tense. However, never forget that when all the fancy pencil work is over, the effectiveness doesn't depend so much on the way you make your promise as on the promise you make.

Right, we have covered some basic principles governing the picture and headline. (I say 'picture' deliberately, because one picture is better than a lot of pictures. If you can simplify the shot to a single scene your ad is working harder than if there are a number of different scenes.) The next stop for the eye is the bottom right-hand corner of the ad. This is where the client's name generally goes, as a signing-off note. Logo-types can speed communication here, but you can also use the space to wrap up the whole of your sales argument in a slogan. I'm not saying that every good ad should have a slogan; often a good case can be made for omitting a baseline altogether, but there are times when it can help. If you do decide to write one, try and see that it isn't just a mildly witty pun, but urges the reader to go deeper into the ad.

Tell what you can't see

Next stop in the eye-journey is at the caption under the picture. There are several hints worth remembering here. First, be sure to say something the reader can't see, never describe what the eye can 'read' for itself anyway. Explain any action that is taking place. Name the characters you are showing, especially if one of them is a well known personality. If at all possible, get the name of the product or service into the caption. If you have a black and white shot, indicating any important colour can be useful. And finally, try to use the caption to direct the reader into the text. For example, a caption could be:

Harry Blank winning the world motor-racing crown.
Read below how X oil helped.

If you have used your techniques wisely, and have kept
the reader's interest so far, you'll have got over a great deal of
information in a very short time. And every part of your ad
has been earning its keep. Let us assume that the reader is
still with you; he will then move onto your cross-headings
and smaller illustrations. Make sub-heads punchy and factual.
Facts sell — generalisations and puffs don't. If you use charts,
make them simple and direct. If you have a smaller photograph tucked into the body copy, caption that as well, using
the same techniques. In graphs and diagrams use comparisons,
name competitors, quote what experts or independent testers
say, or use testimonials from satisfied users.

The smaller print

Finally, the eye reaches the beginning of the body copy. What
are the best techniques to use here? Good body copy *starts in
the middle*. Never begin by repeating any of the story the
reader has already surmised. Go right to the heart of the
proposition, and go with a punch. Never open with the name
of the product — that's dull. Don't start talking about
yourself, talk about the reader and his hopes and desires. And
start with a flip; an up-beat phrase. I once read an autobiography
that opened with the sentence: 'Mum and Dad were married
when I was three'. How's that for inviting the reader to read on?
Remember that the whole purpose of the advertisement is
to make people act, even if that action is simply to stop them
thinking one way about a product and get them thinking
about it in another way. To convince anyone about
anything you need more than specious or weak-kneed argument
and more than unsubstantiated claims and hyperbole. You
need facts. Facts presented clearly, sympathetically and
with inexorable logic — and leavened with a little emotion
— are best of all. Some people say that a copywriter is an
advocate for his client's product. If that analogy is apt, the
jury you have to sway are a hard-nosed bunch, not anxious

to be parted either from their money or their opinions. If you talk to them in clichés, or waffle, or use superlatives that cannot be substantiated, they will dismiss the case without a second thought. You will be guilty of insulting their intelligence, boring them to death, and expecting them to hand over money for rubbish.

The wit to woo

The secret of a good advocate is that he gets attention, then tells his audience facts they don't know. He tells them in an interesting and unexpected way. He gets the listeners nodding in agreement; they say to themselves: 'This man understands me, knows what I am looking for, doesn't treat me as a fool: I will give him a fair hearing'. If people enjoy reading your work, they will go on reading to the end of the ad. Moreover, some of that enjoyment will end up rubbing off on your client's products. Remember, too, you should never set out to write an ad without mustering all the facts. You can't be interesting unless you have interesting things to say, so unless your general knowledge is of a 'Mastermind' standard, never rely on it alone to provide the information.

What makes people read?

You may have heard the old saying that there are only seven plots in the literary world. Countless stories, but seven basic plots. Likewise, there are only about a dozen subjects that make people read. And you will probably find ten of them every day in every popular newspaper. I hold the view that if you take any popular paper for one year, you will have read everything it's ever going to print. From year two, only the people, the places and the numbers of the dead and wounded change. Certainly, I believe if all the world's news dried up tonight, most of our press wouldn't notice the difference. These dozen subjects get attention:

Animals	Disasters	Money	Sport
Babies	Entertainment	Royalty	War
Cars	Fashion	Sex	Weddings

With the exception of Royalty (you are expressly forbidden to feature them in ads), the copywriter can use any of these subjects to help him get over his message. So if you have to talk to young women, you can reach them very simply by using a pretty baby. If you have to talk to young men, often a way to their hearts is through a racy car. I'm not saying that you can pin a subject to a product mechanically, or that originality has no place in your work — far from it — but simply that you will be a better craftsman if you know the techniques.

Here are some techniques you can use to write your ads. These techniques are also used by journalists and editors, who live or die by the number of readers they get. When an editor loses readers, he soon also loses his editor's chair. Advertising people may not be so harshly judged, but failure to make attention-getting ads results in a loss of job in the end. As I have said before, no good advertising is produced in a wild, haphazard or undisciplined manner. The craft of copywriting has to be learned, and the learning involves knowing and practising various techniques.

The WHY technique

WHY is an excellent word to use in a headline:

'Why are American commercials better than your commercials.'

'Why I drive a Rolls-Royce.'

'Brand X motor oil is best for your car. Here's why.'

'An explanation to my fellow managing directors why I must ask £70 for a pair of Church shoes.'

'The Inch War. Why Ryvita helps you win.'

'Why Sarah Jane pulls the boys and Sally Anne can't.'

and so there is a reward for reading. 'Why' allows the copy-writer to present a reasoned argument and list all the benefits the product has to offer. 'Why' makes your ad *interesting*. Let me demonstrate.

Say you were asked to do some work for Signal toothpaste — the one with a mouthwash in the stripes. The mouthwash is a unique selling proposition, so you could be excused if you simply took a shot of a pretty young girl with gleaming teeth and printed your promise loud and bold. 'Signal has a *mouthwash* in the stripes!'. No one could argue your ad wasn't on strategy (it is probably quoting the strategy). Also it's quite clear who the ad is talking to and there is an obvious benefit. But it's boring.

That's where 'why' comes in. All you need do is twist the picture slightly, to show the same pretty girl with the same white teeth, but this time she is with a handsome man. They have their arms round each other, they look into each other's eyes, their lips slightly parted so they might easily be on the point of a kiss (sex makes people read). Then you change the headline by one word: '*Why* Signal has a mouthwash in the stripes'. Now the ad is talking.

Why adds fizz

Another example: let's assume a car manufacturer has sold 10 million cars and wants to announce the fact. You're on solid ground to start with because you actually have something to say. No one could quarrel if you took a nice shot of the car, maybe being clouted by a champagne bottle or something, and capped it with a bold headline: 'Ten million Britons drive a Blank'. On strategy, it makes its point, is talking to drivers, but again, it's boring. But let's say the same ad was broken into various pictures which *demonstrate benefits* of the car; the way it corners, the way it economises on fuel, the way it can carry a lot of people and luggage. You change the headline by one word: '*Why* ten million Britons drive a Blank' and your ad is immediately more interesting and more effective at doing a selling job.

Let me show you again. A manufacturer comes to you

with a washing machine that has some good features, but a pretty stiff price. You decide to add some snob appeal and ask a well-known society lady to give the machine a testimonial. Then you shoot the product in a classy home, with the famous lady beside it and you say: 'Annette Nuttie prefers a Brand X washing machine'. OK, you've carried out the strategy. But judge for yourself how much more incentive there is to *read* the ad — even if you keep the picture exactly as before — if you rephrase your headline thus: '*Why* Annette Nuttie, who can afford any washing machine in the world, prefers Brand X'.

If you simply want to make an announcement you say: 'The men who invented the atom bomb now want to ban it'. But if you've got to *make people read,* you preface all that with 'why'.

The HOW technique

I'd been in the business five years before someone pointed out to me the power of HOW. If your client offers a very complicated product or service and you have a lot of different points to make, 'how' lets you go through them all. But there is virtually no limit to the number of ways the word will work for you.

'How to write a best seller in five minutes.' Who could resist a headline like that (certainly not me, who saw it when I was at Chapter 4 of this book). In fact, it turned out to be promoting classified advertising space and it went through the rules of writing good classified ads. 'How to choose an advertising agency.' That's a pretty compelling headline for a house ad, and any client new to advertising, or a touch unhappy with his present agency, is almost sure to pause. 'How to choose the perfect Hi Fi for your living room.' A generic headline — that is, it could be used by any Hi Fi manufacturer — but it should attract first buyers who want a Hi Fi and don't know what they should look for. 'How to spot a rogue car in a showroom.' I just made that one up, but I know for sure I'd read it and so would anyone else who was thinking of changing his car. Don't these next lines demand that you read on?

> How to read a banana.
> How to have £10 extra in your pocket today.
> How to cut your own hair.
> How to turn the room in your head
>   into a room in your home.
> How to reduce your Income Tax by half.

The cleverest way I've ever seen 'how' used was in conjunction with a stroboscopic photograph (that is a picture where the image is repeated, each time in a slightly different position, so the shot actually records movement). The first image was of a puppy, then the images showed the dog getting older and older until the last one was of a fully grown animal. The artwork must have been compiled over the course of about a year, and you can imagine the impact it had. The headline simply said: 'How to raise a dog'.

The WHERE technique

This is not so much the technique of using a word to begin your headline as thinking of *places* the product can be shown to its best advantage. Ask yourself questions like: 'Where will this product be most useful to the customer?'. 'Where will this product be least likely to work?' 'Where will it perform at its best?' 'Where is it most interesting?'

For instance: a client comes to you with a new kind of anorak. He says it's amazingly lightweight, but also totally windproof. You can show it to best advantage, and it's least likely to work, at the peak of Mount Everest. But that's where it's most needed. So you shoot a climber on the roof of the world, wearing your client's product and have him say: 'This is how I know Brand X anoraks are best'.

Oils are under most duress on race tracks, so that's where the commercials are based. A lady's foundation garment is least likely to be comfortable worn by a dancer doing a zippy dance routine, so that's where to demonstrate it. A safety belt is only useful in an accident, so that's where to show it. Say a manufacturer comes to you with a new wristwatch for women. Not expensive, but not unattractive either, and the selling point he wants to make is, it's waterproof. What about dropping it into a washing machine (one of those with a window in the front). 'If you get into hot water, will your watch give you the time of day?'

The WHO Technique

This is when you ask who can help you sell your product. It can include testimonials, but I want to deal with them under a separate heading, so let us look at 'who' campaigns that are not simply testimonial ads.

You can use virtually anyone in a 'who' campaign. Not just real living people, but characters from history (how many commercials feature Henry VIII?), characters from fiction (think of the commercials that have used Count Dracula, and numerous characters from mythology. One of the best ads I've seen in this category featured a happy little old lady, wrapped in a shawl and sitting in a rocking chair listening to a portable radio. The headline read: 'What Mrs Claus does on that one lonely night of the year!'.

Nor need 'who' be a human being. He can equally well be a star-trekker (remember the Smash Martians), a comic strip character (remember the private eye in the Tic Tac commercials), an animal (the live bear in the Kelloggs Sugar Puffs films), or any of the characters that have been created and made popular by Disney and other cartoonists. I well recall a campaign for butter that featured Mickey Mouse, Donald Duck and Goofy, to name but a few.

'Who' needn't be *one* character either. It can be a fictional family (Katie and her brood from the old Oxo campaign), it can be a group of workers in the client's factory (there is a marvellous ad that shows over 1000 men in white coats standing round a VW Beetle, with the headline: 'It takes this many men to inspect this many Volkswagens'), or it can be any sports team, panel of scientists or members of any group. As an illustration of the last category, I once used The London

Philharmonic Orchestra to promote Hi Fi. I went out and bought one of the orchestra's most famous recordings, and invited the LPO to listen to it played on my client's equipment. I then asked how near to the live performance the recording had sounded and whether the intent of the conductor and players had been faithfully reproduced.

Television actors

A popular technique these days is to invite a well known TV personality to help you advertise. Whilst this can be very effective, it holds traps for the unwary. If you ever ask a comic to do a commercial, be certain he has a funny script. And don't expect always to be able to write that script yourself (you're a copywriter, not a scriptwriter). Arrange for his own scriptwriter to contribute the gags. If necessary, just hand over the sales point (or points) you want to make, and ask him to write his own script round them.

If you hire a famous and beautiful actress to star in your film, don't think that she can carry it without a good idea. A top personality deserves a top creative idea to star in. Only then will you get full value for the vast sum you are probably paying.

If you do choose a TV personality, be sure he/she has a relationship of some kind to the product. It may only be that you want the star's personality to rub off it: check it's the right kind of personality, because once you go through with it, it can last a long time. Finally, before we leave 'who' campaigns, here is one ad that took the idea to its ultimate. It was for a catfood. The food was called 'Miaow' (yes, cats asked for it by name), and the advertiser ran a campaign of grateful letters *from cats* commending the product.

TWENTY MINUTES HARD LABOUR

*A 'who' campaign, after it has been running for some years. Note how it builds on all the advertising that has appeared beforehand, without which it would hardly make sense. Ingenious way to make a mundane product fascinating. (*Art director: *Dave Christianson)*

Twenty minutes hard labour.

For mash get Smash in potato pieces.

The WHEN technique

This entails asking questions like: when will the product
perform best? If you place your commercial *in the past*
will it be more effective? I've seen a beer launched on the
slogan: 'The lusty age is back' with characters in Mediaeval
costume. Could you gain by having the film take place *in
the future*? It was done very cleverly by an airline, who set
their ads in the year 2001, when prices seemed astronomic.
A holiday, they explained, was certainly more expensive
than last year, but it was also cheaper than it would be next
year.

The *WHY* campaign, the *HOW* campaign, the *WHERE*
campaign, the *WHO* campaign and the *WHEN* campaign
are the five basic approaches to advertising. Literally
interpreted they will *not* make you a rich and famous
copywriter. But knowing they exist as techniques will save
you many unhappy hours sweating over a layout pad. Use
the techniques intelligently; add your own 1% of inspiration
and originality, going just that little bit further than the
obvious without getting complicated, and you will make good
ads.

Chapter 7

MORE TECHNIQUES

We've looked at the five basic ways to approach a product; now let's look at some tried and proven techniques which will help you build good ads.

Before and after

Remember the seven-stone weakling who always got sand kicked in his face: then one day he starts on a Charles Atlas course (you too can have a body like mine) and next time he goes to the beach, all the girls are crazy for him? There you have probably the best-known before-and-after ad ever written.

Do you realise how often before-and-after is used? Bald men change into hairy heroes, fat ladies diet down to bean-poles, flat-chested blue-stockings develop Raquel Welch curves, dirty clothes come up bright and stain-free, matted woollens turn soft and lovely, even spotty glassware shines when you drop a little Rinse-Aid into the dishwasher. These examples raise a smile — or at least an eyebrow — listed like that. They seem naive, even childish, and not in any way sophisticated enough to take in customers. Don't let the simplicity fool you: before-and-after ads sell very hard.

The best campaign of this kind I've ever seen is one for Ayds Slimming Toffee. It was written by Ruth L. McCarthy, who even took a credit in the ads; and quite right too, because by giving herself a by-line, she explained why they read so beautifully when they were supposed to have been written by the slimmers themselves. Take a headline like: 'Watch me lose 80 lbs, a picture at a time', followed by a smaller sub-head: 'By Mrs Blank Blanko, as told to Ruth L. McCarthy'. There follows half a dozen snapshots of a heavily overweight and poorly dressed housewife, who gradually loses inches and gains a dress-sense until she's a trim lady with bags of sex appeal. The captions under each picture give her weights in descending order. Then the pay-off convinces you; if she can do it, you can do it. Before your very eyes you have visible proof of the efficacy of Ayds (and the skill of a top copywriter). There are countless other examples:

1   Two beefburgers side by side, one frozen, the other tinned. Before cooking they are the same size. After cooking, one has shrunk.
2   An unplayed gramophone record photographed through a microscope. The grooves are unmarked. The same grooves photographed after being played for 1000 hours. The small amount of wear demonstrates the quality of the stylus.
3   Two car cylinders. One has been lubricated by oil without ingredient XK2. It is scored and dirty. The other looks almost new, since the same motor oil *with* ingredient XK2 cuts wear and gives more efficient motoring.
4   Two plates of buns before a kids' party. Mrs X cooked one lot, Mrs Y the other. Then the same plates after the party. Mrx X's buns have gone, Mrs Y's haven't. Showing that Brand Z cooking fat, as used by Mrs X, gives buns more kid-appeal.

There's almost no limit to the changes you can ring on this old, but trusty, format; you can be serious and scientific, or witty and light-hearted. Whichever approach you choose, done with any skill you can be pretty sure you have a good ad.

Invent a place

There's nothing new about this idea. The big retail stores do
it every Christmas when they build fairy grottoes and install
their private Santa Claus. Local authorities build model
villages to attract tourists. Enthusiastic amateurs build model
railways and a scaled-down countryside to go with them.
And nowhere has it been done with more élan than in
Disneyland, USA.

The copywriter can use the trick. It was done best by
Marlboro cigarettes with their long-running slogan: *'Come to
Marlboro Country'*. Other advertisers soon recognised a good
thing, and Britain was introduced to *Birds Eye Country,* where
vegetables were dewy fresh, and rustics rose with the sun to
pick and pack them in under two hours. Not long after, happy
healthy children were skipping and playing hop-scotch in
Pinta Street, while the milkman delivered an extra pinta per
day. And this was followed by an invitation to us all to come
to *Butlinland* where the girls were pretty, the old folks happy,
hubby downed real ale with his mates, and the kids were
cared for day and night. *Butlinland* was a very good idea,
since it was the only one of all the invented places which
actually existed. And for not too much money you could enter
it and leave your troubles outside the gate for two weeks a
year. A pity the concept wasn't developed with more imagination, as it could have formed the basis of an effective and long-
running campaign. Next, a seafood canner created his own
Ocean, though I can't recall its name. And then they told us
about *Haigland,* the least relevant and most derivative use of
an invented place to date.

As an example of the life still in the idea, consider the
campaign for the airline that wanted to promote holidays.
To emphasise the choice they had to offer, the wide range of
prices, the different lengths of stay and the number of venues,
they called each of their offices *The Vacation Store.* Now
isn't that a good place to buy a holiday?

Invent a character

Think of the long-running campaigns that owe their life to a
character. Katie and her family were in Oxo ads for almost a
generation. Speedy, the Alka Seltzer tablet who starred in
commercials 20 years ago, was recently revived and given
another spell as product presenter. Captain Birds Eye spends
life on the ocean wave stuffing the crew with fish fingers.
Unigate gave us more than a few laughs with their invention
of the milk-filching Humphreys. Never forgetting the eye
patch and The Man in the Hathaway Shirt.

Put the client in the ad

There is a neat little rhyme about what it takes to get approval
to an ad, that goes something like this:

> If the client moans and sighs,
> Insert the name block twice the size.
> If the man is still refractory
> Show a picture of his factory.
> Only in the direst case
> Should you have to show his face.

That being said, there have been some excellent campaigns
based on showing the client's face. One man who stole the
show for a while was wholehearted about it was the late
Commander Whitehead, a handsome bearded gent who
looked like an ambassador, and who Schweppes used in
exactly that capacity to introduce their products in the USA.
Commander Whitehead was no photographer's model; he was
a member of the Schweppes sales force, whose panache and
sangfroid were used to persuade thirsty Americans of the
qualities of Quinine Water and Bitter Lemon. I imagine that
some of the buyers in the big chain stores even met him in
the flesh, so to feature him in the ads as well was very
shrewd. For a time, a Schweppes ad was empty without him.
    Avis used the technique too; twice in fact. Once they
invited customers who wanted to complain to call the Avis

President direct. You could reverse the charges and have a good moan at the very top man. There was a tiny caveat at the bottom of the page. It said, 'If he doesn't answer after three rings, try later'. I wonder how many times he got to the receiver that fast. The second time, Avis used their UK managing director. He made his appeal to the Avis staff to try even harder by publishing it in whole-page ads in *The Times* and other top papers. The gist of the story was: Avis are making big new promises to the public, please be certain we keep them. The ads impressed some people so much that they applied to Avis for jobs.

One last example should be enough to show you the changes you can ring on this idea. Company president, Mr Frank Perdue, appears on American television explaining how much care he takes to raise good chickens and what rigorous standards he applies before he sells them. Mr Perdue comes over as a pretty mean guy who works hard to make every Perdue Chicken as good as it can be. His slogan is: 'It takes a tough man to make a tender chicken'. Isn't it both flattering and reassuring to be asked to buy something by the president of a company.

Give the product another name

The launch of the Volkswagen car into America has entered into advertising lore and I have no intention of repeating any of the story here. But one of the techniques used to make the advertising succeed was to give the product another name, and because that name was based on the styling of the car, it seemed a natural thing to do. What *The Bug* also did was to add a whole new dimension of friendliness, humour and self-effacement to the ads.

You usually invent a new name to enhance produce benefits. For instance, Gillette once introduced a special safety razor blade. Its edge was sharper and made shaves more comfortable. The blade was called *The Spoiler:* imagine the impact of a headline like that with a hand holding a razor blade. The story explained how the blade spoiled your face *by babying it.* (And then you were spoiled for any other blade.)

Uniroyal built a new tyre with road-gripping properties. People really started to want it, after it was christened *The Rain Tyre*. Another tyre company was the first in the States to produce a radial tyre. It was a me-too product (since the Europeans had been building radials for years) until they named it *The American Radial*.

You don't have to stop at renaming the product. You can rename the problem it's made to solve. For example, if you have a worse-than-average headache that needs quick relief, then now have *An Excedrin Headache*. Which is, of course, a headache that only Excedrin tablets can deal with. Or if you have an electric shaver for especially tough beards, a photograph of a chin in close-up, with the bristles looking really troublesome, can be headlined *The Human Jungle* to make the product's performance seem more exceptional. And when Iberia wanted to show off all the planes in their national airline, they headed their ad *The Spanish Armada*.

Comparisons are excellent

There is no better advice I can give you as a copywriter than to say, if you have a better product, *prove it*. And there's no simpler way to do that than by comparison. You simply list the features your product has, and prove, with a checklist, that your competitor doesn't have as many. Or you can compare performance figures and show you product works quicker, or more thoroughly, or lasts longer. Or you can compare the materials used to make your product and show, because you use better stuff to start with, you can offer a better result. You can compare the number of times you inspect your product with the number of times other people inspect

---

SOME BEEFBURGERS LOSE SOMETHING IN THE COOKING

If you want to give your competitor a good knock, compare his product with yours. Then prove the claim that yours is better. Tell in the copy what you don't immediately notice in the picture. This ad couldn't have been made without facts. (Art director: Peter Harold)

Some beefburgers always seem to lose something in the cooking.

Frozen.

Heinz.

Before they were cooked, there wasn't much to choose between the beefburgers above.

Then, alas, the frozen one shrank. So we cooked a few more.

It happened again. And again.

It seems, with some beefburgers you cook, you always end up with less than you expect.

Not so with our canned beefburgers.

There's a full 1lb in every can. They don't come in gravy as some people believe.

And they never promise a meal, then end up a snack.

Once a big burger, always a big burger. That's Heinz.

Bigger Beefburgers from Heinz.

73

What do they say about you behind your back?

You probably won't hear people say these things.

They'll likely whisper them from bed to bed, with you just out of earshot.

But if you become a nurse, the comments that follow will be almost inevitable.

"She's so understanding"

And since you'd never have taken the job unless you liked people, it's understandable they'd say that.

But nursing develops that trait.

It trains you to watch, and listen, and think about your observations.

It's not just a matter of being nice, the people in your care recover more quickly.

"Isn't she confident?"

Yes you will be.

And it will be a confidence based on hard work.

We'll teach you exactly what to do, and tell you why you're doing it, and how it helps.

This complete understanding of the job brings self assurance.

Which you, in turn, pass on to the patients.

Your training is based on many years of experience and millions of case histories.

No wonder it works.

"She's young for the responsibility"

That's probably true.

No other job would have you observing in an operating theatre at nineteen.

Or dispensing dangerous drugs or joining a cardiac arrest team before you reach twenty.

We don't believe teenagers are only fit to dial, file and make tea.

We believe that given the right supervision you can rise to the occasion.

"I wish I could be as efficient."

The whole of your training teaches you to make the most of your time and effort.

In the case of a cardiac arrest four minutes can make the difference between full recovery and permanent brain damage.

Do you think we can afford to let you do anything in a haphazard or unplanned way?

And if you take this efficiency into your private life after you leave work, so much the better.

"How does she keep so cheerful?"

This can be hard, especially if someone has just died on the ward.

(Yes, you have to face the fact you are in a profession that deals with life and death.)

There's plenty of reason to be happy when new born twins appear on the scene.

The knack of acting relaxed, cheery, unruffled is probably learned from the people who've nursed for years.

But it's an invaluable side to any personality.

Are we making you think more seriously about a career in nursing?

If so, why not make enquiries at your local hospital.

Alternatively, drop a line to the Nursing Association.

The Chief Nursing Officer, Dept. of Health and Social Security, PO Box 702, London SW20 8SZ.

Nursing.
It's not just your own life you make the best of.

74

their's. Or you can compare how a 20-year-old item remains perfect when treated with one product, as opposed to a similar item which has deteriorated.

You can compare the price anything costs to buy, the price it costs to run (over any length of time you choose), the price it will bring if you sell it again and the price it will cost to replace if it goes wrong. You can compare maintenance costs, time needed to service, or the skill of the men you have to employ to put it right. So much for product, price and performance.

You can also compare lifestyles. This is an especially useful technique in recruitment advertising, as these examples show. The Metropolitan Police proved that coppers led more exciting, varied and responsible lives than the average man, in whole-page ads that asked: How does a week in your firm compare with a week in ours? The nursing profession proved they could offer more job satisfaction by showing a distinguished consultant discussing a case with a trainee nurse. The headline read: 'Did anyone at work ask your opinion to-day?' The nurses also demonstrated how your social standing improved when you joined the profession by showing a nurse, back-view, with the headline: 'What do people say about you behind your back?'

You can be sure somparison advertising is effective because it is so controversial. Some people will not have it at any price and denigrate it by calling it 'knocking copy'. There may be a case for not knocking competitors because they can knock you back harder. My own view is that if you compare like with like, avoid misleading your audience and don't draw conclusions that can't be justified, it is good salesmanship and common-sense to do comparative advertising. After all,

---

WHAT DO THEY SAY ABOUT YOU BEHIND YOUR BACK?

How to talk to teenage girls. And in doing so, prove that you can offer them more responsibility, and improved status in the community. Here the picture tells you what job is being advertised. Show this ad to anyone who tells you not to ask questions in headlines. (Art director: Paul Hanson)

comparing is what every sensible customer should do before buying anything.

The challenge

This is a technique that crops up every so often, especially to launch a new product. The idea is that the new product *challenges* others on the market and says things like: If you can find a better version of this product, we will give you back the money you spent on ours. Some manufacturers go even further and offer to pay for the alternative that's been found as well. But of course only after they have examined that alternative, agreed it really is superior, and the customer has provided proof of what he paid for it. Challenging slogans include: If you can find a better bourbon, buy it. If you get a better deal in the high street, we'll match it. Never knowingly undersold.

The guarantee

This one is tricky because most of the public is now aware that a manufacturer's guarantee often deprives them of their rights under common law, and that they can be worse off signing it than ignoring it altogether. If you do decide to produce a guarantee, you would be wise to say at the beginning (if your client will wear it) that 'This guarantee in no way deprives you of your rights under the various consumer protection bills'. As for the rest, try to be specific in the items you guarantee, include as much detail as possible (without becoming unreadable) and be sure to stipulate where the manufacturer is accepting more responsibility for the life and performance of his product than he has to under th law. There is evidence that if any mail order ad includes a guarantee, sales are almost certain to be higher.

The torture test

This is one of my own favourites, first, because it can add excitement and showmanship to your campaign; secondly, because torture tests, by their very nature, prove the efficacy of your product; and lastly, because they are not hard to think up. The case of the climber selling the anorak from the top of Mount Everest was a kind of torture test, as was the watch in the washing machine. Here are some others I've used in campaigns.

To demonstrate the efficacy of a self-cleaning oven, we had it painted inside with a mixture of cooking fat, sugar and raspberry jam, which was slowly baked hard onto the oven walls. The 'after' picture showed the oven spotless again, untouched by human hand, and for a cost of about two new pence.

We had a letter from a disc jockey who had stayed awake for seven days and nights, playing non-stop music to get into the *Guinness Book of Records*. The point of his writing was that he had used a Hi Fi set that we were advertising. It led to a very nice shot of an exhausted DJ flopping out over the Hi Fi, with the headline: 'After playing for 168 hours non-stop, a vital part failed'.

One client I wrote for introduced an aerosol bath cleaner and an aerosol window cleaner. We produced a commercial using the first to clean the sides of a white ocean liner, and the second to polish the biggest window in the world (which, if you're interested, is fitted on the front of a horse-racing stadium in Kentucky, USA).

Don't wait for your client to suggest torture tests, dream up your own ideas and suggest them to him. He'll soon shoot them down if they won't work; and if they do work, they make interesting as well as convincing copy.

When words collide

I said a little about putting words together in an unexpected way in Chapter 4, when we looked at The Inch War campaign. It's not out of place to emphasise again here that before you try this technique, you have to decide what you want to say. The effect of seeing words in collision (so to speak) doesn't happen unless they communicate something. For example, I could write CABBAGE SKY, and put two words together for the first (and, I hope, last) time, but since they don't *say* anything, you will simply reject them as nonsense. However, once you know what you want to say, colliding words is part of the *mechanics* of saying it. Everything will become clear as we look at some examples:

> *Soft whisky*
> That sounds a nice idea, doesn't it?
> *Slow ketchup*
> Hmm. I suppose they mean good and thick.
> *Central heating for kids*
> A nice hot breakfast cereal.
> *Try this thirsty hair test*
> Eh? Have *I* got thirsty hair?
> *Bananas: 45 cents a foot*
> They must be joking (the bananas were inflatable).
> *The Tuesday drink*
> Never heard of it, but it might be nice.
> *Table whisky*
> Ah, that's the one good enough to have out on the table when guests arrive.
> *The down-home taste*
> That's the taste you feel relaxed and at home with.
> *Pyjamier pyjamas*
> You mean they make me feel ready for bed.
> *Make a slap-up supper slapper upper*
> I'd like to; tell me about the product that does it.

The great thing about these phrases is they're *unexpected.* That quality makes them seem to be new, when some of the products they talk about are old. They make people read.

You can try the same game with letters. *Drinka Pinta Milka Day.* That is a totally different matter to saying: 'Drink a pint of milk each day'. *Beanz Meanz Heinz.* What a terrific line for a market leader. *Wotalotigot.* Written in kiddy scrawl, it's a way of saying you get a lot of Smarties in one tube. I don't need to point out that large appropriation, long-running campaigns have been built on all these slogans.

Finally, some key words

There is a school of thought among copywriters that says originality comes before all, and while it is no part of my aim to decry originality (indeed I applaud it), I will not accept the collorary that because some words and pictures are used a great deal, they won't bear further repetition. Here, I would like to make it clear that I lay down no rules. There is only one rule about making ads, and that is, there are no rules about making ads. But some words we know are *buzz* words. They provoke a reaction. They include: now, free, introducing, announcing, secret, magic, mother, unique, money off, save pounds, sent direct from the manufacturer, economy, bargain, breakthrough, guarantee, and offer closes today.

I could go on, but that bunch is enough to give you the idea. They are action words and the only qualification to using them is you should make sure they are appropriate. The argument runs, you see, that through frequent use they have become clichés and are, therefore, devalued. Whilst it is true that they are clichés, they still keep their value, as the sales returns never cease to verify. Why they keep their power, I don't know, just as I don't know why people will go on reading newspapers that print the same cycle of stories year after year. But I am sure, and you better believe it too, they *work*.

Chapter 8

STILL MORE TECHNIQUES

You may now have an impression, after the last two chapters, that making ads is mechanical. Not so. There is a parallel in painting. First you learn the craft: how to mix the colours, how to use the brush, how to capture a likeness, how thick or thin to lay on the paint to give a precise result. Then you practice the skills. It's when you are able to add your own inspiration that painting becomes art. And it's when you add originality to technique that ad-making becomes creative. So, more about the craft.

Contests

The best headline I ever saw on a contest ad was: 'For once in your life, enter a contest'. That line recognises that, generally, people feel they haven't a chance in a million of winning a contest, so most of them never bother to try. The others, who feel they can win, are often professional contest-doers, and they have perfected the knack of writing tie-breakers. You see, even if a contest is as simple as a first-form sum, everybody knows that you're going to catch them when it comes to: 'Say, in not more than a dozen words, why you love Brand X'.

Are contests worth considering then? Yes, on two counts. First, they can be a very good way to change the pace of your advertising. Let's say you have a long-established product, with a reasonable sales graph, but somehow it seems to be becoming a part of the wallpaper. If you want to get it back into the public consciousness for a few weeks, plan a contest. The only proviso is, you should have an amazing prize.

Be the chairman of our board for a month.
Own shares in every company on the Stock Exchange.
Smash and grab a jewellers. Keep all you steal.
Stay a week in the Arctic with Eskimos.
Have Annigoni paint your portrait.
Own your own pub.

That last offer is from a campaign addressed to publicans, most of whom are managers or tenants. A soft-drink maker offered to buy a 'free house' for the publican who sold the most of their product in 8 weeks. The contest was heavily advertised and while it was on, ads in the trade press featured different free houses on the market, competitors who were ahead at that particular time, how to win extra points and, one week before the contest ended, a bonus that gave anyone who had fallen behind the chance to catch up.

It's easy to see why the contest was followed closely by the trade. They all wanted to sell that soft drink; some publicans even told customers about the scheme and got them to order the brand. The contest ended, and in one final PR effort, the company held a giant reception where the keys to the free house were handed over and the runners-up awarded their prizes. The organisers then announced plans for another promotion the following year and told everyone to speak to the company reps when they called for more details. That contest earned a great deal of goodwill, prepared the ground for a further year of successful trading and, last, but by no means least, sold a great deal of drink.

The second way to use a contest is to get trial purchases for a product. Say you've got a new line (or an improvement to an old line) and you want a lot of people to try it as

81

quickly as possible. Hold a contest which people can enter only if they send in *proof of purchase*. The way to succeed this time is *not* to offer one big imaginative prize, but thousands of smaller ones, to persuade as many people as possible that they have a reasonable chance to win. (A first prize in a contest like this can't be big anyway, since budgets will never allow it; that scarcely matters if you have, say, 10,000 runner-up prizes.)

The good thing about the second type of contest, from the public's viewpoint, is that it may be possible to forego the tiebreaker; or if you do have to have one, then it can be easier to complete. The bad thing, from the manufacturer's point of view, is that you have to spend a great deal of time and trouble organising the judging. Nevertheless, one advertiser I know who ran the second type of contest got half-a-million people using the product in three weeks.

Mr Ferrari drives a Fiat

Or so I'm told, by the ad I'm looking at now, which is an excellent example of another technique: the testimonial from your competitor. Now it's unlikely that a direct competitor will plug your goods, no matter how much you pay him, but since the man who buys an expensive Farrari and the man who buys a cheap Fiat are almost certain to be different animals, it's no skin off the sports car builder's nose to say nice things about the family car.

Even if you don't have a specific name to drop in your ad (and it's obviously better if you have), you can still use the basic idea.

> The kind of loaf the baker's wife prefers.
> Where travel agents take their holidays.
> Why most car mechanics choose a Volkswagen.
> What other tailors admire about our suit.
> France's top wine taster tells how to choose coffee.

Topicality

At one time you could only be topical in the Press, since only the Press could take copy at very short notice. Then Videotape came along; and now you can have a commercial for motor oil on the box only hours after a driver who uses it has won the World Championship. The benefits of being topical?

1   It's a way to change your pace.
2   It's a way to borrow interest from news, fashion, sport, or current events.
3   It can help the advertiser seem more human.
4   It can let you be very funny.

Topical ads come in two categories. In the first, the advertiser ties in with an event directly connected with his business, e.g. an anorak maker with men who've just conquered a high mountain, or a camera maker with a current photographic contest. In the second, product and event have no apparent connection.

1   When the Post Office raised their stamp prices (again), Volkswagen ran an ad showing the new-value stamp franked by a VW symbol with the headline: 'They are still two of the cheapest ways to cross the country'.
2   When Princess Anne married, Avis Rent-A-Car took an ad showing Westminster Abbey with the headline: 'If you have to be somewhere important today, Avis can help'.
3   When the Stock Exchange Index in New York reached 1000 for the first time, Johnnie Walker ran an ad quoting the figure with the headline: 'Congratulations to those who had the guts to stay in'.

How well have you read this book? Test yourself

1   Where should the product be when you write an ad?
2   What's so helpful about an advertising strategy?
3   What technique is used when an ad features a film star?
4   What single word is most likely to increase readership?
5   Name three subjects that make people read.
6   Of the 1500 ads seen daily, about how many register?

They are still two of the cheapest ways of crossing the country.

This is a timely reminder from VW that a Beetle can do 38 miles to a gallon of 3 star.

40,000 miles to a set of tyres. Often 100,000 to an engine. That it never needs anti-freeze. Hardly ever needs oil. And holds its value like few others in Glass's Guide.

So that even at £989 for a basic model, a Beetle's a bargain.

So is a new 3½p stamp, if it's used properly.

If you stick one on an envelope and address it to Volkswagen (GB) Ltd, Volkswagen House, Purley, Surrey we'll send you a Beetle brochure. Absolutely free.

Few things in life work as well as a Volkswagen.

Rec'd retail price VW1200 £989 inc VAT and Car Tax delivery seat belts, number plates and currency exchange surcharge extra.
VOLKSWAGEN-GB LTD. VOLKSWAGEN HOUSE, BRIGHTON ROAD PURLEY SURREY TELEPHONE 01-668 4100 A MEMBER OF THE THOMAS TILLING GROUP

The quiz (or test) technique is a favourite with editors. Think back to how often you have checked to see how good a lover/husband/wife/driver/parent you are? Since the format is so hard to resist, use it in ads too, but with a word of warning. This kind of ad is almost always generic; the headline can apply to almost any product in the category, so unless you really are stuck for something to say, you should try to be more specific.

Range advertising

As a general rule, putting a range of products into one ad is a *bad* idea. Because:

1   People never buy a range.
2   The time to say there are variations in your product is *after* you've convinced me I should buy the general concept.
3   Equal emphasis on many products means scampy treatment for them all.

I advise you to either persuade your client to spearhead only one of his range, or to feature the different variations in separate ads.

If the client does agree to spearhead one model, the question then arises, which? Generally, the answer is the one that sells best. Or failing that, the most expensive, because it presents the product-type at its best, and any glamour and style can rub off onto the cheaper models.

If you're dealing with the fashion trade, apply a different rule: by all means spearhead your most popular line, but also take one ad to show your most outrageous garment. When

---

THEY ARE STILL TWO OF THE CHEAPEST WAYS TO CROSS THE COUNTRY

*Here's how to make a picture really work hard. And be topical. And change the pace of your advertising. Note how this ad builds on all the other VW ads that have appeared before it. Lesson: you very rarely advertise in a vacuum. (*Art director: *Derrik Hass, from an idea by John Knight)*

a fashion editor looks at the season's creations, she goes for the zany, the wild extravaganza, to put in her column. It may be true that only a very few customers (maybe none) will ever buy that garment. But they'll say: 'Did you see that marvellous dress by so-and-so?'. And they'll feel great if they can tell you they are also wearing a so-and-so creation, albeit in a much more conventional style. When the House of Schiaparelli re-opened in Paris in 1977, designer Serge Lepage offered a white chiffon dress with 512 diamonds sewn into it. Price? — two million dollars. I don't know if he found any buyers, but he certainly won a lot of publicity.

What about the techniques for making range ads? There are at least two. One is the *guide technique:*

> For a range of girdles and bras: 'Every girl's guide to a lovelier Silhouette'.
> For a range of haircuts: 'Your guide to the hairstyle that best suits your face'.
> For a range of frozen foods in winter: 'Your guide to the week's best vegetable buys'.

The other is the *what do you want most?* or the *which is right for you?* approach. Here, you group the products according to the qualities they offer, and invite readers to decide which variation suits them most.

Quotations

This is often the place where the trainee copywriter starts — and believe me, it's a mistake. Famous poets and dramatists rarely have much to say about selling. There may be times when an apposite quotation works better than anything else, but they are few and far between.

Here are two instances where quotations were right. When the US Government was urging Americans to come to the polls in 1969, one ad summed up the message with a quotation from Edmund Burke: 'All that is necessary for the forces of evil to win in the world is for enough good men to do nothing.' Who could refuse to vote after that warning? And when Christian Aid wanted to push home their belief that a helping hand is better than a hand-out, they said: 'Give a man a fish and you feed him for a day. Teach a man to fish and you feed him for life.' When you think of the number of advertisers asking for charity these days, you won't find many better reasons to give than that.

All that said, when I began as a copywriter, I wasted many hours looking through Roget's *Thesaurus* and the *Dictionary of Quotations,* hoping those books would lead me to good headlines. It never happened! Much better to follow the routine from Chapter 2: study the product, study your market, get all the facts you can, decide who you're talking to, then *think*.

Demonstration

Showing the product at work is one of the most common (and most effective) ways to sell. It is best when you have sound and music to help you, which means making a film. But it is also possible to demonstrate in press, either with stroboscopic pictures (the ones that capture movement) sequences of photographs (before-during-after) or with diagrams. For example:

> Four pictures each captioned with a time: 10 a.m., 10.1 a.m., 10.10 a.m. and 10.11 a.m. In the first picture, a man is standing beside the open bonnet of a car holding a hosepipe. In pictures two and three the hose is pouring gallons of icy water into the engine. In picture four, the car is driving away. Headline: 'A little bit of moisture never hurt a Volvo'. Not quite so effective as it would be if you saw a film of water splashing over points and plugs and gushing round the distributor, but effective enough.

If you *are* working on a film, there are four basic ways to go:

1 Show-and-tell The best British example of this technique in recent years is the TV commercial for the Black & Decker

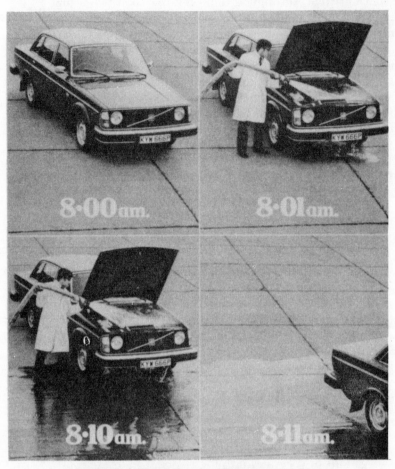

A little moisture in the atmosphere won't stop a Volvo.

What you see happening in the photographs actually happened.

The Volvo started first time, leaving behind a relieved photographer and a smiling spokesman from Volvo.

Not that anyone should have been surprised.

The vulnerable parts of the Volvo engine, like the plugs and distributor, are well-protected from the elements.

Come rain, hail, sleet or snow, a Volvo is expected to start.

In Sweden, temperatures can be sub-zero for 6 months in the year, and being stranded on a country road within the Arctic circle isn't quite the same thing as waiting for the AA outside Cheltenham.

The Volvo 244 is reliable because it has to be. And because it's built to be.

It takes a Volvo nine hours to crawl through

the final assembly plant.

And in a factory where engineers outnumber stylists by 40 to 1, each car is minutely examined.

But if you're looking for statistics to back up our reliability claim, one seems more convincing than any other.

92% of Volvo owners intend to remain Volvo owners when they next change their car.

And as evidence goes, we'd say that was pretty reliable. **VOLVO**

For your free copy of "The Volvo Facts" write to: Volvo Concessionaires Limited, Lancaster Road, Cressex Estate, High Wycombe, Bucks. HP12 3QE. Tel: (0494) 33444.
Export enquiries to: Volvo Concessionaires Ltd., 28 Albermarle Street, London W1X 3FA. Tel: (01) 493 0321.

88

'Workmate'. We see that versatile tool put through its many practical uses (saw-bench, step ladder, vice, and so on), and the film ends by showing how neatly 'Workmate' hangs away on a garage wall. No tricks, no star actors, no silly jingles, just straight voiceover, telling you what you see and how much you have to pay. Excellent selling.

2 *Slice-of-life* Action in this kind of film opens and ends on 'real-life' situation, but in the centre of the film, the advertiser drops in a demonstration, e.g. open on housewife holding her head.
Husband: Headache, dear?
Wife: Something dreadful.
Husband: You need two Blank tablets. Dissolve to transparent plastic model of human head. Dotted arrow animates from mouth to back of head while voiceover explains that Nothing acts faster than Blank. (OK I'll have nothing.) Dissolve back to wife, now smiling.
Husband: You look better now, dear.
Wife: Oh yes, Nothing acts faster thank Blank.
And we cut to a close-up of the pack, two tablets, and a title. I know it's a cliché and utterly boring, but you see films like it on the box almost every week in winter, so they must be doing something right (mustn't they?).

3 *Trick films* This is exactly what it says, using cinema tricks like slow motion, so the audience can see what usually happens too fast for the eye to follow. Or repeating a few frames over and over again to emphasise a point. Or reversing the film. Or changing from colour to black and white (or vice versa) for the demonatration sequence. Or by shooting through a microscope, or using X-ray shots, or any other device which can help you prove a point.

A LITTLE BIT OF MOISTURE NEVER HURT A VOLVO

Here is a demonstration and a torture test combined. Plus a picture that proves the claim being made. And how's the headline for under-statement? (Art director: *Phil Mason*)

4 . *Animation* This is where it's impossible in practical terms to film the product in action. Say you have a tyre that stays inflated if you get a puncture at speed. You can't film it patching itself from the inside; you can explain using animation. By the same token, you can't wait around filming how the action of plaque causes tooth decay. But you can simulate it well enough through animated drawing.

The keynote of demonstrations is simplification: say it clearly, say it believably, and don't leave any loopholes.

A lot can happen in a day

Using the word 'day' can help you produce a slogan:

> Make the day, with Cadbury's Milk Tray.
> A Mars a day helps you work, rest and play.
> Players (cigarettes) add pleasure to the day.
> One of today's great tastes.
> Bournvita puts back what the day takes out.
> Spend a day with the Princess.

So we can learn two things: first that the word 'day' can add weight to a slogan. And you can make a good ad if you base it on a day in the life of the product. There are other uses too. The Saturday Shirt was a very good brand name for a range of leisure shirts. The Tuesday Drink formed the basis of a campaign for whisky. (The story was you could drink it whenever you liked, but you *had* to have some on Tuesdays.) And I offer the idea of an aftershave called Friday to any

---

WILL THE REAL COFFEE YOU SERVE THIS SATURDAY HAVE PART MISSING?

Remember 'Help the two of us'? Here's another example of how cutting something in half adds impact. It turns the expected picture into the unexpected. The whole campaign was based on a fact that came to light only after talks with the Lyons chief coffee blender.
(Art Director: *Paul Hanson)*

Will the real coffee you serve this Saturday have part missing?

Most ground coffees can't give you; their all, because they're roasted wastefully.

They let the aromas, the flavour and other coffee goodness escape.

Not so at Lyons.

We roast our Original Blend in a different way. Under pressure.

So the very essence of the bean is preserved.

With Lyons you get all the bean. More of the aromas and flavour. And more of the goodness.

And what other coffees can promise you that?

Fresh Ground Coffee
Roasted Under Pressure

91

manufacturer who wants it. (Get that Friday feeling, every day of the week!)

The strip cartoon

Speaking personally, I'm a sucker for strip cartoons. My eye will find one in an acre of newsprint and I've upset more than one fellow tube traveller by trying to read a strip over his shoulder. The one I know off by heart is about the teenage girl with dandruff (or worse) who can't go to the Ball. Her best friend recommends Product A. She uses it. And Bingo, here we are at the Ball, dancing with Billy the Gang Boss, who then whisks her away on a ton-up motor bike, the dandruff-free tresses blowing in the slipstream. Thinks: Thanks to Brand X I pulled the Leader of the Pack.

Before you use a strip, decide who you're talking to: of course, it's good for kids, but it's also not wrong for our two million barely-literate adults. One final hint: hire a well established strip cartoon artist to draw your ad for you; it's not as easy as it looks.

Chapter 9

TELEVISION

Most, if not all, of the techniques covered in the last three
chapters can be used whether you are making an ad to
appear in the Press or on the large or small screen. But since
paper and film are two very different media (David Bernstein,
in his book *Creative Advertising* actually lists 29 points of
difference between them), I have given film a chapter to
itself. There is only one difference I want to stress — and I
freely acknowledge it is included in Mr Bernstein's list:
1   A newspaper ad cannot *make* the reader read.
2   A TV Film has a much better chance of *making* the
     viewer view.
   Anyone who has walked into a room when the TV is on,
and noticed how, almost against his will, it attracts his
attention, will understand what that means. The small screen
grabs you despite yourself, and though you may be totally
uninterested in what is going on, or even sceptical about
what is being shown and said, you are still, very often, forced
to keep looking.
   This ability of TV to make the viewer view can sometimes
act as a deciding factor when you are in two minds as to
which of the media — Press or the box — is right for a
particular product. I would make the following rule-of-
thumb. If the product is in a low-interest category — that

means if the product has nothing intrinsically interesting about it — then probably the best medium to use, other things being equal, is television. If, on the other hand, the product is interesting in itself, then quite likely the best place to put the ad is in the Press. Now I know as soon as you read that you will be able to think of half a dozen examples where exactly the opposite is the case. So let me stress, this is only a rule-of-thumb, and all other factors should be equal — which, of course, they very rarely are.

Use TV for low-cost goods

There is, however, a good argument behind it. There is little or nothing of genuine interest that you can tell an audience about sweets, canned fruit, pet foods and most shampoos, deodorants and hair sprays; they are all low-interest category products. And whenever budgets permit, their agencies promote them on TV. On the other hand, there is a great deal to be said about new cars, washing machines, Hi Fi equipment, digital watches and shares in unit trusts, and the best ads for these products generally appear in the Press. It is also worth noting that the second list — of high-interest category products — is also a list of expensive products that people buy only after a gestation period, when they mull over the different brands in their minds. So another rule-of-thumb may be surmised: the more the product costs, the less likely it is to be an appropriate subject for a TV ad.

Cut your script to the bone

Let us now turn to one very basic principle in making a TV script. You would be well advised to confine your film to one main thought or promise. Even if you bought the whole commercial break, you would only have two minutes to tell your story. And you may be unlucky enough to have to cram it into one slide and 7½ seconds. The most common time length is, of course, 30 seconds. So keep your script simple. Do not, under any circumstances, prepare a lengthy and learned argument which meticulously sets out the case for your product. You simply won't have the time to put it over. Hit your audience with a single thought. And only use enough words to back up that thought in such a way as to make it believable.

For example, commercials for Ryvita Crispbread say: 'In the Inch War, Ryvita helps you win'. And supporting that claim is the evidence that no matter what other kind of slimming bread you buy — starch-reduced or whatever — not one has fewer calories. Then they leave it at that. They do *not* say Ryvita has a terrific taste, costs least of all crisp-breads to buy, is made exclusively from natural foods, contains no additives or preservatives — nothing, in fact, except salt — comes in different varieties and is the most popular brand in the country, selling more crispbread than all the others put together. They *could* say that, for it is all true, but in the context of a 30-second TV commercial talking to slimmers, it's simply not relevant.

Say something simple

This rule of only putting in your commercial a single thought may be hard for a client to swallow, especially when, as in the case of Ryvita, the product has an excellent story to tell. But you must try to make it clear to him that the average TV viewer — and we are all average TV viewers, however out-of-the-ordinary we may feel — simply won't remember more than one thought from your commercial. And this is not because he or she is stupid, but because they couldn't care less about commercials, pay very little attention to them, have a healthy scepticism towards them and, expect for the most part, only to be entertained by them. And if you want people to have a message in their minds two or three days after they have seen your spot, and are pushing the baby round the supermarket with a million other claims attracting their attention, then say something simple.

If you do have a complicated sales message and feel — and you may be right — that you can only do justice to the product if you tell its full story all at once, then TV is no place for you. Either you go into the Press, or you go on the box with what I call 'cross-reference' commercials, which simply direct people to read your ad on a certain page in the *TV Times,* or to write or ring for your brochure which will tell them all they need to know. If you do 'cross-reference' ads, leave the address or telephone number on the screen long enough for the viewer to write it down. And remember he probably hasn't got a pencil poised over a notepad at that particular moment.

The more pictures, the less words

Here is another rule-of-thumb about TV writing. If the picture is complex, the words should be minimal. If the message is complex, then the picture must be very simple. On no account should you have a fast-cutting, tension-building picture, overlaid by a wordy message. It's impossible for your audience to follow both. To give you an example: I once wrote a commercial for a glue manufacturer, in which a table was glued upside-down onto the ceiling. A rope ladder hung from the table and the idea was to have an 18-stone man climb the ladder and sit inside the table, then throw down a weight which was attached to the table by a rope. Visible proof that the glue on the four slender legs was strong enough to carry the man and withstand the shock. Since the audience would want to see if the table was going to come unstuck, all their attention would be on the picture. So there could be no question of having a lengthy voice-over explaining how the glue was ideal for a thousand-and-one sticking jobs.

One picture, lots of words

At the other end of the scale, Cunard shipping line, when they wanted to tell people about some special reduced rates and revised sailing times for their flagship, had a commercial consisting of one shot: the QE2 sailing past a stationary camera. Five seconds looking at the picture was enough to establish all there was to see. Thus the audience could concentrate on the voiceover and there was a good chance they could take in the various prices and dates. So remember: dramatic pictures need little or no words. Complex messages need simple, easy-to-assimilate pictures.

Steal

In previous chapters, I have had no hesitation in recommending that when you are making Press ads you steal as many techniques from newspaper editors as you can. Naturally, the same advice applies when you are making a TV script. Slow motion, quick cutting (there is now a law which says you must not have cuts shorter than four frames), laying the soundtrack of one scene over the video of another and all the other tricks of the film trade are constantly being refined and embellished by the top directors and film editors. The TV director of the production company you use will certainly be well up on all the latest filming devices. Unless *you* keep up with them, there can be a danger that your scripts become old fashioned. So be aware of the movies: be certain to see the films which innovate and, more especially, those which draw the crowds, because today's 'in' film may well contain some techniques which can help you create tomorrow's 'in' products.

Demonstrate

The great forte of film is, of course, demonstration. I do not intend to repeat here what I have said about the tremendous value of demonstration, but let this be another rule-of-thumb for you: if you think the product will benefit by demonstration, then that is a strong argument for using TV. And demonstration includes mechanical, comparatives, side-by-side, exaggerated graphics, i.e. The White Tornado, and, of course, emotional benefits. Visible proof, before your very eyes, that the product works, and you can see *how* it works, is a sure-fire way to sell. That well known ad salesman Harry

Wayne McMahan has a showreel of 100 demonstration commercials which he is constantly updating and which, for a large fee, he will bring in and show to your creative department. If you can afford his prices, you could do a lot worse than benefit from his collection.

Dialogue is more interesting than voiceover

Some people believe that the slice-of-life film is television's most effective advertising format and certainly, if the benefits you want to put over are mainly emotional ones, then there is little to beat the playlet that can have you laughing, crying, and loving the product all in 30 seconds. There is no small skill in writing these playlets for you need an ear for dialogue, an ability to condense which outstrips the sub-editors at Reader's Digest, and a keen sense of humour, as well as the talent to dream up distinctive characters. If you can do all that — and I don't think that those sort of skills can ever be fully taught — then slice-of-life commercials can make your products, and probably yourself, famous.

Name campaigns

Another great ability of TV is that, very quickly, it can make the viewer remember the name. I can only recall one Press campaign that really pushed home the name of the product, and that was the Schweppes campaign which *never mentioned the name* at all. It simply said 'You know who' and, of course, we all did know who. But on TV it is done year in year out. Remember the launch campaign for Tuc crackers, those little biscuits suitable for so many occasions, which were backed by a song lyric of 'Tuc Tuc Tuc'. And the power saw ripping through wood, steel, abestos, plastic sheet, laminates and the rest, with the voice pounding out 'Black & Decker, Black & Decker'. I even saw a motor scooter film which had teenagers zooming across the countryside to a soundtrack of 'Vespa-pa-pa-pa-pa'. The 'pa-pa-pa' being,

of course, the onomatopoeic popping of the exhaust. So
the technique of registering the name seems simple enough.
All you have to do is say it over and over again for the length
of your commercial. But nicely!

Ladies and gentlemen, the Presenter

Next, that good old standby, the presenter commercial. Those
of you who remember the launch of commercial television in
1951 will recall how we used to be subjected to presenter
commercials night after night. The film would open with a
fresh-faced man, sitting behind a sign saying 'Marketing
Manager', who would hold up the product and gush about it
until you were perfectly bemused. He'd said too much, he'd
said it too quickly, he'd said it unconvincingly, and he and
his ilk soon became very boring. If you thought this meant
the death of the presenter commercial, you were wrong. It's
just that the presenters got better, more famous, more
cleverly disguised (some became cartoons for instance), or
they appeared in situations which stopped you from
recognising them as presenters at all. One film worked
brilliantly, because the man started off: 'Here I am in this
kid's stomach ...' whereupon a toffee the size of a tea chest
fell from the roof narrowly missing his ear. It was apposite
and very funny, but it was still a presenter commercial. Later
a film opened in the middle of Death Valley with parched
and cracked earth as far as the eye could see. A guy walks
into the frame and explains how the dead earth has a
parallel with dead skin and how a certain soap can help
stop you skin dying. An incredible venue, a fascinating
story, an ingenious analogy, but still a presenter commercial.
And finally, there is the commercial of the man who appears
on the ladder of a pier, covered in the grease and gear of a
cross-channel swimmer. Only he has a hamburger in his
hand and starts raving — and I mean raving — about so-and-
so's Green Relish. You're fascinated, you can hardly believe
it, you grin, and maybe even laugh out loud as he falls back
into the ocean with one mighty splash. Highly momorable
and intrusive — but a presenter commercial.

Jingle jangle

And now a word about jingles. I have to admit I have to
admit I have never written a jingle in my life. I have also
noticed that jingles go in and out of fashion and that you can
have a year when the commercial breaks are filled with them
followed by a year when you probably never hear one. I have
no doubt that many of my readers can quote case histories by
the dozen proving that jingles work. I can even remember *one*
jingle, although I haven't heard it for about 20 years: 'You'll
wonder where the yellow went, when you brush your teeth
with Pepsodent!'. If you must have a jingle, I recommend that
you go to the people who specialise in writing them. If you
say the right thing and set it to the right kind of music, it's
likely to set a number of cash register bells ringing. It's just
that I can't get out of my mind that famous line about
jingles:

If it's too stupid to say it, sing it.

Finally, before we close this chapter, a paragraph or two
about using famous personalities. I have said most of what I
want to say under the heading of WHO campaigns, but one
or two points are worth reiterating. If you are going to spend
a lot of money on a famous personality, you must be sure he
or she is right for the product. That's probably an easy thing
to decide, although you must always be prepared for the
account person or client who, when you suggest a name, says:
'OK, but what happens to your campaign if he dies?'. If you
are sure the guy is in a good state of health, has clean morals
and is not likely to get involved in a fight in a night club, then
you should be certain to have a contract that says your
personality won't do similar commercials for a rival product
within an agreed period. And not only for a rival but, if you
can afford it, for anyone at all.

Stars fade if the script is faded

Having signed up your star, that is not the end of the story; you've got to write a good script. If you are dealing with a comedian, let him help provide his script with the single thought written in. If you have a beauty like Ms Brigitte Bardot, don't think all you've got to do is let her simper; give her something sensible to say. If you use a character actor like Arthur Mullard — who in my experience never fails to come up with the goods — give him the right dialogue. He told me once that he earned a living for the first 10 years of his career by saying one line only: 'I'll knock your bleedin' block orf'. Accompanied, of course, by the shaking of a fist the size of a ham and the other guy disappearing over the horizon. Arthur is worth better dialogue than that nowadays — and gets it!

If you do pay for a personality, use him or her to the full. Many's the time I have seen commercials where half-a-dozen other characters, none of them recognisable, share the screen with the star. This is wrong since the personality of the man — which is what you have paid so much for — rarely has the chance to come over to full effect.

Quite often, there is a tendency to hire well known personalities to do voiceovers. Being the sort of guy who likes to get value for money, I am tempted in situations like that to preface the script with 'This is Sir Laurence Olivier speaking'. If you don't say so, only one listener in a million will ever know. It's also not a bad idea, unless your hero is of international fame, to *title* on who he or she is.

The lure of the screen

If you are at the beginning of your career and feel that you are particularly attracted to writing for television, make a good friend of your agency TV producer and ask his advice on your ideas at an early stage. When he tells you that you can only get 60 words into a 30-second commercial, please believe him. And then write only 45 words (or less) because that is enough to have to listen to and assimilate in so short a time.

If you do make TV your forte, you may find you don't excel to the same extent in the Press. Not to worry about that, at least for the first years of your business life; better to be great in one half of the media than only mediocre in both. On the other hand, you may find you are most at home writing for the Press. Fine, do your utmost on paper before you try to master celluloid. The best copywriters are out-standing in both, but they are few and far between. My advice in the early stages is to go for one half of the craft and master that to the best of your ability, catching up on the other part when you know the rules and when and how to break them. But don't base your initial decision on the supposed glamour of mixing with the famous and watching the actual filming at exotic locations. In my experience, there are few things more boring than taking two days to put 30 seconds of script into a can, even if you sweated blood over every dot and comma. You can find just as much satisfaction reading your work, concisely written and properly laid out, in the pages of any paper or magazine.

Chapter 10

TALKING TO THE HOUSEWIFE

Housewives spend most of their money in the high street;
creative people spend most of their working lives in comfortable offices (if you're a critic of the advertising business, you
say 'Ivory Towers'), and the most common accusation levied
is that ne'er the twain shall meet. I shall answer the charge
in good time. At the moment, however, it is enough to point
out that whatever level you work at in the creative department,
from director down, you will find a great deal of the advertising you make is aimed at women. And it won't take you more
than a few months in an agency to realise that the products
which command really large appropriations are bought
mostly by housewives — cars, beer, petrol and oil being the
only exceptions I can think of.

Because this is so, most of advertising's critics condemn
the *way* we talk to housewives. Some say we caricature them
and turn them into domesticated little biddies, scatter-brained
sexpots or creatures whose life is dominated by the desire
first to catch, and then to keep, a man. It is claimed we talk
down to women and that the inanity of some of the promises
we make insults their intelligence. It's true that many of the
women in TV commercials *are* caricatures. But why? Because
creative people use cliché characters as a kind of shorthand

You know how it feels if your nails aren't right.

But do you mumble the favourite excuse "I haven't got time for fussing with nails?"

Well, now you've no excuse.

Just For Nails, from the makers of Cutipen, is the new, easy way to nail beauty.

Each product has been carefully formulated to help get nails looking good. And, more important, to keep them looking good.

Short or long. With or without nail polish.

You'll find Just For Nails if you go to Boots, larger chemists, and department stores.

And the sooner you go, the sooner you can get your nails looking right.

All the time. JUST FOR NAILS *Cutipen*

to indicate the category of person the product is for. Since you have only 30 seconds to make a sales point, you can hardly build up an original and many-faceted character in your ad. So you use a cliché; and if the cliché is a home-loving little biddy, at least it tells the viewer who the merely explaining it.) Once in a while a really clever creative person devises a series of slice-of-life commercials where the leading lady does develop a character ('Madge' in the US Palmolive ads is a case in point). But advertising writers with the skill to create like that, and clients with the courage to buy creations like that, are few and far between.

In defence of women

Some of our critics say advertising exploits women. Talk down to, yes; deprive of helpful information, yes; insult their intelligence, yes; we do all that to women in our jobs. But I believe women have been around long enough and are tough enough and canny enough to look after them-selves, and most journalists who claim otherwise are simply on the lookout for copy. One of the world's religions preaches that women, poor creatures, do not have souls, but even it concedes that they might have brains.

So how should you make ads addressed to housewives? Rule one: give plenty of facts and all the relevant information you can lay your hands on, right down to simple things like the sizes and washing instructions. Rule two: never make a claim you wouldn't expect a woman you know *personally* to believe. If your wife would reply 'You must be joking' to a headline, then so will everybody else's wife, unless you

---

YOU KNOW HOW IT FEELS WHEN YOUR NAILS AREN'T RIGHT

Remember the technique of putting the product where it's least likely to work? This is a similar technique: instead of showing what it's like when you use the product, show what it's like when you don't. And what a nice change from all those expected shots of beautifully manicured fingers. (Art director: *Nick Wilcox*)

believe you married one of the few intelligent women in the country. Rule three: steal techniques. I've already told you to copy newspaper editors and film directors; you should also copy the editors of women's magazines. Like everybody else in the communications business, a lot of the time they use techniques. Put this book down for a moment (if you can bear to) and pick up any women's magazine; the chances are you will find at least one item on each of the following: cookery, fashion, knitting, make-up (or hairstyles) family health and the best way to care for your husband.

Not forgetting, of course, the obligatory love story. I don't mean this as a criticism; women's magazines simply print what most of us want to read. Here are some subjects that — if you present them with any glimmer of freshness — will never be boring.

Pictures that pull

No matter how often photographers shoot them, or papers and magazines print them, very few ladies tire of pictures of babies. No one has cashed-in on the phenomenon better than Pears Soap, who've been running their beautiful baby contest for more years than I can remember. Don't let that put you off — if you have to sell almost any product for babies you'll have to go a long way to find many things more grabby to illustrate.

The same applies to weddings. We keep albums of our own wedding photos all our lives, and there is something about a bride and groom that will fascinate most ladies. Is she pretty? Is he handsome? What are they wearing? Hasn't her mother got a funny hat? The best man looks worried, doesn't he? How many commercials have you seen based on someone's wedding day? Give yours a new twist and you're pretty sure to get attention. If babies and churches work, then put the two together and have a picture of a christening; you won't find many women who can't identify with that.

I've already said something about how journals handle fashion. It's not unknown for an advertiser selling, say, built-in kitchens, to get enquiries not about the product, but about where to buy the dress that the housewife was wearing in the ad. And finally food pictures are always interesting, especially if the dish is new and colourful; remember the principle taught to all good cooks — we eat with our eyes.

Recipes

Look in any women's magazine and you'll find a recipe. So why not use one next time you make a Press ad for a food product? Research proves recipes increase readership; if anyone ever tells me they want to put one of my food ads into a reading-and-noting test, I always drop in a couple of recipes. Having said that I give you a warning: don't fool with this technique, or use it carelessly. Never accept a recipe unless, first, you have had it tried out by a qualified home economist (many big food companies have one) and, second, you have eaten the result. There is no surer way to get the housewife to hate you than to get her to make a recipe and find, after all her preparation and cooking, the meal is terrible. Moreover, there are plenty of housewives who can judge whether or not a recipe will work *before* they try it, and if what you suggest sounds stupid they'll turn the page with a snort before you've even started to plug your stock cubes or whatever. What's more, you'll lay yourself open to a barrage of irate letters from disappointed ladies; and if they write to you, instead of the editor of the magazine your ad appears in, you can count yourself lucky. If any editor *does* catch you publishing grotty recipes and crucifies you for it, he's only doing his job. And trying to get you to do yours.

Money-off coupons

The best time to use a coupon is when you want to persuade housewives to *try* a product for the first time. Unless this is your aim, I am sceptical about whether coupons are worthwhile. Not because housewives don't cut out coupons; of course they do. But many retailers resent those little bits of paper because they make a lot of extra work collecting and redeeming them. Not only that, it can sometimes be very difficult for a manufacturer to ensure that his coupon is exchanged in part-payment for his product, despite what he prints to the effect that it must be so used. Some big stores will take coupons in part-exchange for anything you buy, so the only effect a coupon has is to help the housewife knock a few pennies off her final bill. Which won't do your client much good if his product remains unbought.

However, bearing in mind the casual attitude of many shop keepers and the difficulty of pinning the coupon to the goods offered, coupons still give you a few other benefits. They can help to improve the product's position on the shelf. They can encourage folk to buy a larger size of an existing product, since the coupon makes the bigger pack obviously better value for money. You can use coupon in specific areas, to boost a TV campaign in that same district. And since not all coupons are ever redeemed, your client can appear to the retailer to be giving away a lot more promotion money than he actually is.

As far as writing coupon ads is concerned, I think you should try to *headline* that there is money off, even though you have to say how much in the coupon. You should position the coupon on the part of the page where it can be most easily cut out, and to do that you should check with your media department whether you have a left- or right-hand page insertion. If your coupon offers very little, say a penny or twopence, acknowledge the fact in the body copy, not forgetting that every little helps. Above all, keep a sense of proportion; there are few things more laughable than the manufacturer who gives away peanuts and allows his agency to make it sound in the ads like he's offering gold blocks. If the client criticises your copy on the grounds that you haven't made his offer sound big-deal enough, ask him how much money it would take to make his own wife rush for the scissors.

Free samples

There is no stronger ad than the one that *proves* the claim it is making. And one way you can do that is to offer a free sample so the customer can put the product to the test for himself.

I once wrote a campaign for a no-calorie sweetener, where the claim was: 'It leaves no after-taste'. The product came in multiples of 100, but the client also made packs of only four individual sweeteners for use in restaurants. Since his production line was already geared up for these tiny quantities, I suggested that readers could send for a free sample, which was, of course, the four-pack. This is a good example of how it pays the creative person to find out all the facts about the product: it would have been quite impractical to offer a free sample if you had to give away 100 sweeteners at a time.

There is a natural instinct in account people to dismiss free samples on the grounds of expense. Always check before you leave them out of your armoury. If a free sample proves totally impossible (and there can be many reasons apart from money) a good alternative which I think is under-used in Britain is 'scratch-and-sniff'. This is where a small piece of paper is impregnated with the smell of a particular product (a perfume, a new soap, a new fruit drink) and the paper is then glued to the page in the magazine in which your ad appears. To release the smell, the reader scratches the impregnated section with a fingernail. I've always wondered why none of the men's aftershave manufacturers haven't used this technique, say, in ads appearing three or four weeks before Christmas. At the other end of the spectrum, a really appetising smell could help to sell canned sauces or those foil sachets of herbs and spices which turn weekday stew into boeuf bourguignon. It's even more appropriate in these cases because you can't tell what the stuff is going to taste like until after you've bought it, while with the aftershave, at least you can ask for a sniff at the shop counter.

The point about free samples and 'scratch-and-sniff' is that both techniques offer you the chance to give the customer some *experience of the product*. If somebody doesn't like the way your sauce smells, you might lose a customer but, as I never cease saying, you can't please all the people all the time.

Economy sizes and value for money

This includes everything to do with making the housekeeping go further, which is a major task of many of the women you'll be talking to. SALE advertisements should be brief and to the point. They should show the product, the old price, the new sale price, and the amount of money saved. Opening times of the store are vital and if the quantity of the item on offer is limited, you must say so. No flowers of speech or arty alliteration: give 'em the facts.

Economy sizes, if they are economy, should give the quantity and specify in cash terms how much better off the housewife is if she buys the larger size. If a new pack is being introduced for the first time, flash it with a money-off deal, for a limited time only. New packs are also a good place to reiterate your product story. Even old packs should be crammed with product information and offers pertaining to the product.

If what you're selling is cheap, never be afraid to say it costs less than Brand X. Some clients are squeamish about words like 'cheap' and 'bargain' and don't like to sell their products on a price story. Most of the time this is nonsense. Sure, you'll probably lose the man who thinks expensive means better: he's going to buy the most expensive anyway, and very often more fool him. But you can also lose people who want value for money if they don't know that's what you offer. If the product is new, a price advantage can be very important indeed; if it's been around for some time then maybe the price flashes on the supermarket shelf will do your good-value job for you.

If you give 20 biscuits or slices of crispbread or spoonfuls of coffee or ounces of jam in your pack, and the competition gives less, shout it to the skies (provided always that price-for-price the competitive story stands up). If your kids' shoes last longer, or your trousers have two layers of material in the knee, make a big benefit of it. Best of all, give a wear guarantee. And never be scared of having a reputation for charging less than most.

If you do have to charge the most, cram your ad with information, line drawings, graphs, percentages and beautiful,

beautiful facts, which most of the time the housewife is
starved of and which she badly needs if she is to convince
her husband and justify to herself that the hefty price you
are asking is worth paying.

As far as stretching the housekeeping is concerned, information is what the housewife wants most together with real
efficiency and real economy. They are the keynote to selling
detergents, scouring pads, air fresheners, insect killers, polishes,
window cleaners, even the major purchases like washing
machines, dish washers, 'fridges and vacuum cleaners. They
should all be extremely efficient and not cost too much,
either to buy or to run. They should be incredibly reliable
yet backed by a professional repair man. If they do break
down and can't be repaired quickly, you'll never make a sale
under that brand name to the same person again.

The beauty business

Cosmetics, face creams, skin-care products, slimming aids,
shampoos, conditioners, hair colourants and even hair sprays
are, for the most part, sold on a minimum of information. So
what happens? The buyer reads the rest of the story on the
editorial pages of her favourite magazine, which is prepared to
go into full details about the 'do's' and 'don't's' of how to
tint your hair, how long it will last, how easily it will wash
out and how much practice it takes to get it right. And if the
editor tells the story, he's not going to pull any punches if
your product isn't right. So, first, get it right and, second,
tell the story yourself. Don't say women aren't interested:
you can hook them on a new slimming aid or a new shampoo
as easily as you can hook a man on a new car or a new beer.

If you have to sell any of the products listed above,
remember the techniques in Chapters 6, 7 and 8. Demonstration of how it works (for hair colourant) and how easy it is
to do, is meat and drink to most women. The experience of
other housewives is also always good to relate; I don't
think anything can beat commercials showing how women
swear by their own brand of detergent, however boring we
men believe them to be. Every lady, however dowdy, is

interested in fashion. Ads that explain how to make a dress yourself, be certain of a perfect fit and save money into the bargain, also have an appeal.

If you ever have to launch a new fashion, you won't go wrong if you pin it to a fashionable personality. A woman who is known for good taste and good dress sense can be a marvellous asset to your client if he wants the world to wear a new look he has created. What the Queen wears is always interesting. What film stars wear and fashions that appear in films also have a good chance of catching on. (Remember the Great Gatsby look?) Hairstyles too are always good news.

The following advice may be old advice but it's worth repeating. When you write to women, remember not to write to a category. Ask instead: Will they *believe* what you say in your advertising? Will they be interested in the way you're saying it, and have you answered all the questions likely to arise in their minds including how much your product costs (so many advertisers nowadays leave out the price), and where to get it? I've only this minute put down a magazine with an ad promoting a new toy: it sold me on the basis of how much pleasure it would give my child, but forgot to mention how much I'd have to pay for it, where I could find it, and even omitted a manufacturer's address or phone number, killing any final hope of getting further information. These are crimes I hope no one will commit after they have read this book.

Women aren't dull, so don't you be

When he was at the start of his career, the French intellectual Jean Cocteau asked what was the secret of success. 'Astonish them', advised his mentor, and that's sound advice for the aspiring writer. Many of today's best-known copy and art people made their names by slaughtering sacred cows. At one time, for instance, it was death to be funny in advertising ('Nobody buys from clowns' ran the old adage). But now, as you know, viewers are disappointed if a commercial doesn't make them laugh.

Before Alka Seltzer was relaunched (in the USA), the

pundits swore ads for medicines had to be straight-faced. They also swore that brand-names were sacrosanct; then somebody wrote the slogan: 'With a name like Smuckers it's got to be good'. For decades, agencies positioned products as the very finest of their kind; then a writer realised what a rich vein could be mined from the idea that a product that was *second* in the running had to try harder.

If you want to win yourself a reputation, *astonish*. All the guidelines are fine, but when you know and understand them, break them. For instance, when Selfridges needed a SALE ad, but didn't want to list any of the goods in the sale, they ran a marvellous page addressed to the queue in Oxford Street. 'The street washing truck — they warned — comes round at 3 a.m.' Now and again, say to yourself: I know who I'm talking to: I know what I want to say: I'm gonna say it like no-one ever said it before.

Chapter 11

HOW TO JUDGE YOUR WORK

In a sense this is probably the most important chapter in the book. I am going to list seven criteria you can use to decide whether you have made a good ad. But a moment's thought will show you that this is not simply a checklist; it sets a standard to which all your work should aspire. I call these criteria the seven silver rules for judging creative work: silver rules, because there is only one golden rule, and that is 'there are no rules when you create advertising'. If you apply these rules — as and when they are appropriate — you will become a good copywriter. If you ignore them, or feel that some are too harsh to apply, then you'll always find someone saying 'could do better'.

But first a word of encouragement to the trainee who reads the list and feels he's never going to be able to make ads that live up to it. Don't forget you are learning your craft; nobody expects you to be brilliant after only a year or so at your desk. Like the author, playwright or scriptwriter, you will only become proficient through practice. If I have learned one thing in our business it is 'the less you do, the less you want to do'. And if you sit around in your agency sidestepping jobs you will soon find you have lost the inclination to make any ads at all. *So be hungry for work.*

Nobody in any office is busy all the time; if, during one of those lulls, someone asks if you're interested in taking a brief to help out a colleague, grab the chance. Even if it's only to do a run-of-the-mill trade ad, there are still countless ways trade ads can be done differently, and it is a chance to practice. Your creative director and the account people will soon recognise a willing worker. You will be given bigger and better chances. When you get briefed to make an ad today, it might take you a long time to assimilate the facts and produce an idea; persist, apply the seven silver rules, and before too long you will be able to field anything anyone throws at you.

The urgent copy date

The biggest problem most young creative people have is dealing with deadlines; it is a fact of life that advertising is geared to copy dates and you will find that often you are asked to work very fast. The agency management should have impressed on the account people the importance of giving you as much time as possible; if one particular account person makes a habit of bringing you panic jobs, the best thing to do is ask your creative director to put matters right. But, I must emphasise, there is no profit in worry. (I once met a guy who believed he was paid to worry. What nonsense. He was actually paid to keep a level head and stop other people from worrying.) You will never produce your best work if you are screwed up with worries and tensions. The more relaxed you are, the better your brain will work. It is because I understand how easy it is to worry over deadlines that I have described in such detail the *practical* steps that will lead you to ideas.

Feeding your mind with facts about the product, the customer and the medium you're going to use is like fertilising soil. When you've got enough information to work on, solutions begin to grow almost automatically. The best antidote for worry is to busy yourself finding out all you can about what you have to sell. When it comes to making ads, there is no substitute for application.

115

But enough of this preaching, let's get to the seven silver rules. You remember how I told you it was a good idea, when you had made one or two ads, to pin them on your office wall and give them the 'overnight' test? Well, when you come into the office fresh next morning, here are the seven questions to ask:

1 Is it 'on strategy?' You might think this criterion is so obvious as to be not worth mentioning: you'd be surprised. You see, sometimes when creative people are at work, they come up with a brilliant solution — except that it's not in line with the strategy. Never mind, they think, this idea is so good that we might persuade the client to buy it despite the fact that it's not what we planned to say.

Ninety-nine times out of a hundred when this happens, the creative team are being propelled by their own (quite natural) enthusiasm; a brilliant idea is only brilliant if it's saying the right things. This is not to say that there has never been an occasion when an outstanding creative solution has brought about a revision of the strategy; far from it. But you must be careful, before you go back to change basic thinking, that you're doing it for the right reasons.

Most strategies should be written so they isolate the main thought the advertising campaign has to communicate. (Turn back to page 40 for a reminder of how strategies are composed.) What you have to ask is whether your ad has hit that main thought firmly on the head and put it over in the tone of voice that the customer likes to hear. If you answer 'yes' to that question, then your work is 'on strategy'.

2 Is it clear who you're talking to? By now you're probably tired of reading the question *who are you talking to?* But if you only remember one thing from the whole of this book, that is the one most worth remembering. There isn't a newspaper or magazine editor, a playwright, an author, a film director or a composer who doesn't know who his audience is. They all decide, first and foremost, who they are writing for, and note this — none of them tries to write for everyone.

You know who's going to buy *Yachting World:* you know

the audience *DIY Magazine* reaches; you certainly know who *Woman* is for. The *Sun* never writes editorials to impress readers of *The Times*. The best feature-film director in the world never tries to please everyone. The man who composes a pop tune writes for a different world than the man who composes a violin concerto. Every one of them knows that if you try to reach everyone, you get no one. It is vitally important that you make this clear to your clients, who understandably feel that the bigger audience they reach, the more goods they will sell. It isn't so.

> *If a feature film can't please everybody, if a novel can't please everybody, if music by a great composer can't please everybody, how can one ad please everybody?*

My first boss put it at its most basic: 'If you're selling wooden legs, the headline's gotta be: "To all one-legged men".' Well, I don't entirely agree, but the principle is right. There is a school of thought that says if you're talking to young men, show young men in the picture; if you're talking to older women, show older women; mothers, show mothers; brick-layers, show brick-layers, and so on. If you're not certain of the kind of person to illustrate, it's a good rule-of-thumb, though I can't promise it will make you devastating ads.

3   Is your ad interesting?   Think about it; can you really expect anyone to be interested in a dull ad? Is the piece of work you have pinned to your wall telling the reader something he doesn't know? Does it look like it's going to inform? Or be fun to read? Is it the kind of ad that will draw you deep into the body copy? Is it going to keep you going as long as it keeps going? Does it offer a clear reward for reading? The questions are so logical, yet it's perfectly obvious from work that appears every day in the Press (and on the box) that not many creative people ever ask them.

Some products are actually dull products. I've explained what to do then — use showmanship. One thing you can be sure of; if you find the ad boring to make, the world will find it boring to read (or watch). The only way to get an audience enthusiastic is to be enthusiastic yourself. Nothing irritates me more than to see creative people tackle an ad with an 'Oh God, I suppose I've got to do this' attitude.

And it's no good putting up the excuse that although most people find a subject uninteresting, there are a few who are fascinated by the product and it's only them you're trying to reach. Some people do plough through ads despite the creative teams' efforts, but that's no credit to the copywriter. Remember this: as far as creative people are concerned there should be no boring products, no dull companies and no unimaginative sales pitches: only dull, boring, unimaginative advertising.

4   Is your ad instant?   The average ad has about 1½ seconds to say 'We've got something for you!'. That's how long the reader pauses over it, considering whether it's worth his while to read on. We can learn a lot from this. Firstly, if the promise you are making hasn't come across in that 1½ seconds, then it'll never get across. Nobody reads on into the body text of an ad if they haven't grasped the proposition in the headline and picture. (Yes, I know you can capture attention with trick and shocker headlines, but they almost invariably let the reader down when he reads on to find what they're about.)

It's good policy therefore to look on your Press ads as posters. You know a poster has to make sense without any body copy; ideally a Press ad should stand up to this test too. Body text in a Press ad is to back up your main thought with relevant facts. You try to arouse a wish in the reader to own the product. Then you convince him that he'll benefit greatly and any money he spends will be a wise investment. Then you tell him what to do (visit the showroom, fill in the coupon, ring this number now). But the big promise has to sing out straightaway. I would like a pound in my pocket for every time I heard a creative team justifying an oblique headline by saying 'Ah, they'll understand as soon as they read on!'.

5   Is your ad believable?   Sometimes creative people can be very strange. They can write down a piece of nonsense on a layout pad and, because it rhymes, or has a neat beat to it, they think the style — plus the fact that it will shortly appear in print — will make it incontrovertible. Yet if you took those very same words and *spoke* them to the creative man concerned, he'd scratch his head and tell you not to be so daft. Some copywriters can put dialogue into the mouths of characters in commercials that would not be out of place in a lunatic asylum. Let me quote an example (this is not to take a knock at the advertiser concerned, or indeed the creative people concerned; it's simply taken from memory at random to show you exactly what happens). A TV campaign has spent a lot of money telling us that 'Mellow Birds will make you smile'. (The claim is too stupid to say, so they sing it.) But if you walked up to the copywriter who wrote that line, with a jar of the product, and said to him, 'This coffee will make you smile', he'd say: 'Why? What's funny about it?' Bird's Mellow Coffee will please, possibly. It might win compliments for its new taste. It might lead someone to ask for a second cup. It might get you a name as a discerning coffee drinker. But there's one thing not even the finest Jamaican Blue Mountain coffee has ever done to me, and that is make me smile.

What happened is that the creative team got into their office that morning, shut the door, and disappeared down a secret tunnel into Adland. And in Adland people go round in ecstasy at the mention of the product name. They believe promises that a child of five would think preposterous. And they talk a language peppered with words like exciting, unique, greatest and best-in-the-world. Now I know you, dear reader, are not among that type of creative person; you are quick-witted and intelligent (or you wouldn't be reading this book). But I mention the existence of Adland to make certain that you never go there, for it is a crazy place where people will believe anything, despite the fact that it is transparent nonsense. Make your work believable; don't *kid* yourself you believe it, or other people who are not so discerning as you will believe it. Ask yourself: is this genuinely credible?

6 *Is your ad unexpected?* Is that question unexpected? Then maybe you have always made ads the expected way, when being unexpected can increase the impact of your work

tenfold. Since it is your job to make ads, you probably spend a great deal of time reading ads made by others. Have you noticed how there are some ads you instinctively avoid because *you know what they are going to say?* You can repeat the promises off-pat; the copywriter can start a sentence and you can finish it for him. The most obvious example is cigarette advertising, where copywriters are reduced to a 20-word vocabulary (taste, value, flavour, best, finest Virginia — add the rest yourself, there aren't that many). An unexpected interpretation of a selling claim can make a £100,000 appropriation feel like a £500,000 appropriation.

Here is something I have discovered about how to produce unexpected ads. First, you go through the usual process — learning about the product, the market and the media. Then you make your ads; you work hard at them and put them on the wall for the 'overnight test'. Then you forget about them for maybe three or four days. Sometimes it's quite a good idea to turn to a different job altogether, just letting the main thought of the ads on your wall rest under the surface of your mind. (Don't worry over it, or dig it up to look at it; leave it there and let your subconscious work on it for as long as you have time available.) If you're lucky, when you come back to your work, a quite remarkable thing can happen; the unconscious thinking you've been doing can suddenly show you a completely new way to make the ad. Your brain has been at work without any direct help from you; all you did was feed it the facts, produce a few expected ads, and let those efforts lie under the surface of the mind.

This 'seeing with new eyes' can also happen if you've taken the trouble to write body copy for your ads. Re-reading it, you may well find that about three-quarters of the way through there's a phrase or sentence which throws quite a different light on what you're trying to say. You can put this to the test now; pick up any newspaper you like and read through half-a-dozen quite ordinary ads. I'm prepared to wager that down in the body copy, where few people go, there's a line that — if it had been spotted — could have brought the ad to life. I understand that one reason why this line so often remains unused is that the creative people are so pressed for time that they haven't a chance to let the work lie for a 'gestation' period. It's worth telling people who ask you to work at express speed that in the end they only get the advertising they deserve.

7   *Has your ad proved its case?*   Proving an argument isn't just the best way to make a sale; it's also probably the most difficult thing any ad can do. There are plenty of cases, of course, where a claim can't be proved. *Beanz Means Heinz. Happiness is egg-shaped. Central heating for kids.* How do you go about providing proof for slogans like these? But a great number of claims can be proved. When the Metropolitan Police set out to recruit for the force, they proved that a policeman's life was more interesting, responsible and rewarding than almost any job offering a comparable income (and many paying a lot less).

When the COI ran ads to recruit nurses, they proved a nurse was a girl you would trust with your life, a girl whose opinion was valued even by hospital consultants and whose contribution to an operation could be crucial. Another ad, which invited readers to place their finger on the headlights of a car, proved how easy it was to be unseen in fog (when the lamps disappeared so did the vehicle).

If you are looking for ways to prove your claims, seek out people who can give independent advice. Your readers know that if the manufacturer says something, he's saying it because he wants you to buy his product — and what's more, he doesn't mind exaggerating a bit to make a point. But when an independent scientist, or a motoring correspondent, or a satisfied user, or *Which?* magazine says something, it isn't the manufacturer talking and you have a much better chance of being believed. Bloggs Brand isn't best because Mr Bloggs says so. But if Mr Bloggs' chief competitor admits that old Bloggs doesn't make such a bad product, that's real reason to buy.

So there are the seven silver rules to apply when you are assessing your work. If a new ad or campaign meets all the criteria, then you should have a block-buster that breaks every sales record in the book (remembering always that the quickest way to kill a bad product is with outstanding advertising). One more piece of advice. It would be no bad thing if you made this checklist public; in other words, showed the account people you work for how you assess an ad before you hand it over to them. Since very few people have any idea at all about how to assess creative work, the fact that you have a pretty rigorous system should carry some weight. If they know that the work they take to clients complies with these silver rules, they can use the knowledge to help sell the work, because the rules show that the work isn't top-of-the-head stuff, but has been produced by craftsmen working under a discipline. The rules make sure the ads are saying the right things to the right people in the right way, and what client will turn down work that can promise all that?

Chapter 12

HOW TO DEFEND YOUR WORK

When you decide to become a creative person in advertising (and there are few more interesting jobs) you have to recognise that probably two-thirds the work you do is never going to appear. The very nature of the job means that every ad you make has a great many hurdles to jump before it gets presented to a client, and then, very often, your troubles are just beginning. A very talented art director once told me that if he managed to end his working year with three campaigns, either in print or on film, he counted himself lucky. Three campaigns a year may not seem many if you are a young enthusiastic writer ready to graft all the hours of the clock to build up experience. But after 23 years in the business, the work that I have to show, including campaigns which I have now discarded because they are dated, amounts to considerably less than that. So you may as well learn to accept, as early as you can, that even ads which you consider to be among the best you have ever made will, as often as not, remain forever in layout form. If you can keep that thought in mind, and also be careful to cultivate a sense of proportion (by which I mean that although making ads is your work, they are, after all, only ads), you will have a happier working life than if you expect everything you do to sail through the system unopposed.

Let us look for a moment at the hurdles your ads will encounter in their journey to the public eye. The very sternest critic you will ever have to deal with should be yourself. A first thought may indeed prove to be a best thought, but do not be content with it from the outset. Cross-check that the ad says with crystal clarity who it is talking to.

Showing work to your boss

Be certain you are saying exactly what you want to say, and saying it in the right tone of voice. If your ad comes up to scratch on these criteria, then try it on your creative director.

Remember, it is his job, his *raison d'etre* almost, to maintain creative standards in the agency, so he will probably be the second-sternest critic of your work. You must hope that he is judging it from a background of experience and with an almost instinctive knowledge (a gut-feel if you like) of whether it will do the job for which it is intended. If he says 'no', don't throw a tantrum or drop into the pit of despair; sound him out as to how he thinks it can be improved, and if you don't take every word he says as gospel, at least give his suggestions a fair hearing. Remember that if he says 'yes', then it goes to the account people (the next hurdle) with all his authority behind it; the responsibility for its efficacy has moved from you to him. The account people will bombard you with all the doubt they think the client may have. Yes, they are second guessing his reaction, but remember again that they are the guys who took the initial brief and be patient if they voice suggestions as to how your work might be improved. Please don't fight for every full stop and comma in the draft copy. Rarely has any piece of copy that I have written passed through the system totally unscathed.

The next stop is the plans board, which is generally held whenever there is a major new batch of work going through the agency. For a plans board you should muster all your facts and have a full knowledge of the product and the customer ready at your fingertips. Very often you can be made to look foolish if someone pops up in the plans board with a set of figures or an attitude unearthed by research of which you were not aware. (Not that this should ever happen, since it is the accounts people's *duty* to be certain that every relevant piece of information has reached your office, even before you put pen to layout pad.) If your work goes through the plans board, it means that the whole agency has put its authority behind it. This is a point that account people should bear in mind during the client presentation; whatever the client says, a body of highly experienced advertising people has studied the work and in their opinion it is doing exactly what the marketplace calls for, in the best way they can imagine.

Meeting the man who pays the bills

By now you are ready to meet the client; you have been through all the questions he could ask and presumably you have good answers to them. In client meetings you should be wary of any show of irritation or impatience. Your work will stand a much better chance of being accepted if the client sees you not just as a creative person but a responsible business person who understands his problems, and acknowledges that you are spending *his* money. If he can look on you as a friend as well as a business associate you will have a much better relationship than if he learns to see you as a protagonist. You will never win a war against a client, because in the last analysis he has the right to say 'no' to a campaign; he pays for that right by contributing to your salary.

One question the wise creative person asks himself when he comes up against fair opposition in a client meeting is: 'If it were my money that were being spent on this advertisement, would I still go ahead and spend it?'. That's a sobering thought and one that will bring any sensible creative man down from a pitch of indignation when the client queries whether a particular phrase used to express a sales point is quite as clear as it might be.

You will probably find that the client is several people

and you will not always have a chance to sell your ad to them all at the same meeting. The lower ranks of the client's hierarchy are often the toughest to get through, since (unhappily) they may also be second-guessing and want to pre-empt their boss's comments by making them themselves. Patience and logic are your weapons now; never throw them away in favour of temperament. The final OK may rest with someone as high as the managing director. It is not his job to be able to tell good ads from bad ads, it's your job. But that doesn't give you the right to say 'I'm the professional — you've got to accept my word'. Quite the opposite; you've got to be logical enough and articulate enough to *prove* that your work is right. If every managing director could distinguish good from bad, there wouldn't be any bad ads around. No one either, inside or outside our business, would deny that today bad ads actually predominate.

I hope these last pages have helped explain why three campaigns a year is an acceptable success rate. And whilst I have tried to stress that level-headedness is the best help in selling campaigns, I do not intend that you should present your work with a mouse-like timidity — not that I've ever met a mouse-like creative person. I could fill a book triple this size with criticisms you might meet in your working life and still not have covered half of them. But since there are some which constantly crop up — and have no substance when looked at in the light of common-sense — I list them below, with some arguments to refute them.

What if you run it without the sound?

This is a trick the old-hand account person will sometimes try to pull on you when he is judging your TV storyboard. He looks at the pictures to see what is being shown; he reads the words to see what is being said; then he asks if anyone will understand the commercial if you turn off the sound. I don't know how this criterion was first arrived at; I suspect it came into being when someone realised not everyone gives 100 per cent of their attention to commercials. Then they said to themselves: 'If we show the same thing as we tell, we'll capture more customers'. There are three ways to counter this argument:

1   A stand-up comic, the world's greatest opera singer and a fine musician are all dead if you turn off the sound. All the subtleties of humour, tone of voice, nuances that suggest product benefits, the additional qualities that music and laughter can give your commercial are lost by asking if it works in silence.

2   Anyone not giving their attention to what is being *said* in a commercial is almost certainly also not giving their attention to what is being *shown;* so you've lost them anyway. Although TV companies may charge you for every set switched on at any time, you will never get everyone in front of a TV to give you their undivided attention all the time.

3   The simple fact of life is that viewers *don't* turn off the sound. And some of the best commercials gain their force from a juxtaposition between words and pictures. I would say that any commercial that can be understood completely with the sound off is only half a commercial, and should be rejected on that criterion, rather than be found acceptable on it.

Nobody reads body copy

You've got to be careful of this one, because if your message doesn't come over after people have seen the headline and the pictures you've got a bad ad, so it's no good saying they'll understand when they read the body copy. That's when it's quite true that nobody reads body copy. But if your picture and headline tell the story (or part of it) and you then expand on the benefits, you are on sounder ground.
   Nobody reads *bad* body copy; that is copy that waffles, lacks facts, is badly constructed and gives no reward for reading. But people do read good copy. Say you are doing an agency house ad (and those are very often the hardest to make) and you write a headline: 'How to spot a *bad*

advertising agency'. If there is room under that line for hundreds of words, anyone on the lookout for a good agency will almost certainly continue to read the ad so long as it tells him things he doesn't know.

The question 'How long should an advertisement be?' is the same question as 'How long is a piece of string?'! There is no *rule*. An ad is too short if it ends without saying the right things to make a sale. An ad is too long if it repeats itself, gets boring, stops giving facts and information, or uses two words when one would do. If you want a guideline on how to judge what the right length of any headline, baseline or piece of body copy should be, then consider its *content*. If that is right, the length isn't often wrong.

Mrs Bloggs won't get it

This criticism is very common. You show an account person your ad, he smiles, nods sagely, rubs his chin for a couple of seconds and says: 'Ah, I get it, but will C2 housewives in Wigan?' implying that, as an intelligent, highly paid ad man he is *au fait* with the nuances and sophistications of the big city, but dull old housewives north of the Wash are totally mystified by Monty Python, Porridge, The Two Ronnies, any serialised classic, indeed any TV show which rises above pavement level. And consequently, your ad must appeal to the lowest common denominator or it is a dead duck. The common result of a criticism like this is that you produce ads that ignore intelligent people, thereby encouraging intelligent people to ignore your ads. There is a common belief in our business that the majority of the population are simpletons. I hope you will have gathered enough from this book to know that I refute the belief and state that, on the contrary, almost everyone in the world knows something you don't, and advertisements should, if anything, write *up* to people rather than talk down to them. But note well: this is *not* an excuse for writing ads that Mrs Bloggs genuinely won't understand.

Any product could say that!

Go to work on an . . . you were going to say egg, weren't you? But the copywriter could just as easily have said 'bacon sandwich' or 'bread and cheese' or 'Scotts Porridge Oats'.

The fact is, eggs said it first, so anyone who says it second is simply helping to remind people of the original slogan. The same applies to The Inch War. It was said for|Ryvita, but it could equally well apply to any slimming product. The simple fact is, a product without a unique selling proposition can have a unique selling *personality*. So as a creative person you have to decide whether there is something unique and relevant you can say about your product; if there isn't, then go for a generic campaign and do not knuckle under to an unthinking critic. If he persists and refuses to admit that scores of products are using slogans that could equally well have been used by their competitors *provided they had thought of them first,* then you will have to ask him outright to define the USP for you. If he does it, you're wrong; but if he can't, then he should shut up and be glad you have created a personality that the client can make his own.

Our competitor uses that word!

This criticism is really sneaky because it implies that the creative people have been stealing someone else's work. But it is still commonplace. Your client makes beautiful furniture, and you say so. Then you come across an ad for A. Smith which says his furniture is beautiful. Oh dear, you can't use the word beautiful because Smith's have already used it. They've also used lovely, attractive, pretty, appealing and desirable, so you can cross out all those words too. The only guy who should be pleased about that is Smith, because you have, at a stroke, granted him a monopoly on all those words and gagged yourself into the bargain. The rule here is simple to follow; if you are making the same claim as your competitor, then that's the time to rethink. But if the sense of what you are saying is quite different, then it matters not one jot, and indeed it might even be inevitable that you use some of the same words. I would add that you should apply common sense, but very often when ads are being judged, common sense is in very short supply.

Don't say it isn't so; they might think it is

This is really a Catch 22 situation. Say you are advertising a book club. Now the problem with book clubs is that people think they will be under the obligation to buy a lot of books. So the writer puts in a clause about 'no obligation'. Ah, says the account person, mentioning there is no obligation will make people think there *is* one. Or again, your ad carries a coupon which assures readers that if they fill it in, they will get literature but no one will call. Ah, they say, isn't that suggesting that someone *will* call? Or again, you put in a clause that promises money back if not satisfied. Ah, isn't that suggesting they might *not* be satisfied? Well actually, no. Not unless you believe that if the ad says 'available in white' people will actually believe the product is available in black. Words mean what they say, and if a customer feels he may be under an obligation, or that someone will call, or that he may not be happy with whatever he has bought, it's only sane to reassure him. I think the only riposte to comments like that is to ask the offender whether be believes that if you say the product is good, people will actually believe it's bad. And when he says 'yes' (which he will) then ask him why he is advertising at all.

You should never ask a question in a headline

The only answer to this nonsense is to find a really terrific ad that has a question as a headline, stick it down on a large piece of cartridge paper, and headline it: 'Why is this ad wrong?'.

It's not a women's magazine ad

I once made a campaign for a product bought by women. The obvious medium for it was the women's magazines. But the art director, clever fellow, made the ads very graphic; the photographs were brilliantly simple, the type was beautifully set and the visuals, finished off with acetate, looked as though they had come out of *Nova* magazine (may it rest in peace).
We presented them to the client. He fell for the proposition right away and thought we had done a marvellous job interpreting the strategy. But, he went on, they don't look like women's magazine ads; they look like they came out of *Nova*. Can't you make them more in keeping with the medium they'll appear in? Now pause there, dear reader, because you are in a very dangerous position of making the client look a fool, which is not a wise thing to do. So in the most delicate way possible you have to ask him whether the ads, when they appear in *Woman* and *Woman's Own*, will stick out like a sore thumb. An when he says 'yes', say 'good'.
And now a few words about some criticisms you *should* pay attention to.

It's ad-y

That could mean your advertisement looks like an advertisement, sounds like an advertisement and is in every way just what people expect an advisement to be. Can this be bad? Yes, because people are inclined to disbelieve advertisements and to ignore every piece of print that looks like an advertisement. So the criticism 'it's ad-y' is a non-cliché way of saying that your whole ad is a cliche. Strange though it may seem, ads that don't look like ads can be a very effective way to get attention.
There was once a technique, used very well by the Milk Marketing Board, of making ads that looked like the beginning of a piece of fiction. They contained the same kind of illustrations and the same typography that the women's magazines used to present love stories. And, of course, they appeared in women's magazines. This technique

is now expressly forbidden (more-the-pity since magazines have become duller for it) but you can see the principle. Making an ad look like a part of the editorial, provided it is done intelligently, can increase initial readership. Ad-y-ness also means using the usual terrible cliche phrases that crop up time and again in the work of third- and fourth-division agencies. You can repeat off-by-heart the claims that will appear in Building Society ads, for instance, puns like 'your money is as safe as houses', and all those boring promises about security and earning good interest, as if we didn't know that the interest rates are identical in every Building Society in the land.

It's expected

This is a very similar criticism to the last, but I include it because some creative people are surprised that their work should strive to be unexpected. They think, for example, that a perfume ad isn't a perfume ad unless it looks like a perfume ad. The real craftsmen know that unexpectedness is part of making ads; they will go to extremes to find a new angle on an old promise. And that doesn't mean just finding new words to express an old thought. 'It'll help you get your man' is not the only thing you can say about perfume, just as 'It'll help you get your woman' is about the most boring thing you can say about after-shave lotion. So once you know who you are talking to, don't just plump for the thing you think they want to hear.

I was once given the job of promoting a fizzy drink, made, as it happens, with real fruit. Not much real fruit, but at least more than you get in Coke or Pepsi. The account people wanted me to go out on the theme 'made with real fruit' (surprise, surprise), but not only was the claim boring, there was so little real fruit in the fizz that it was totally unbeliev-able. Instead I suggested a campaign to persuade mothers to include a can of the drink in their kid's satchels every morning. Free school milk had just been discontinued and the kids were looking for something to sip in the morning break. So instead of commercials shouting 'Dring Pop, it's made with real fruit', we ran ads saying 'Put a little bit of fruit in his satchel' and 'A little bit of fruit helps restore pupil power!'. You don't ignore the obvious claim, you just try to make it unexpected.

It's boring

In all my time in the business I haven't yet found an answer to this one. It's the hardest of all criticisms to answer (yet surprisingly, it's one that is rarely levied at you by account people). They will often buy an ad that could send a reader to sleep on a bed of nails, provided they think it's 'the right message'. But very often the obviously right message is wrong because it is so obvious.

I think the best way to decide whether or not an ad is boring is to ask yourself: 'Would I read it?'. That may not seem to be saying much at first glance, but think back to what I said about subjects that are intrinsically interesting (cars, entertainment, drunkenness, contraception, road safety, careers) and products that are uninteresting (soaps, baked beans, steam-baked bread, canned fruit, ice cream, chocolates). If there is nothing you can say that is unexpected about the product, remember the rule: showmanship! Get some interest from somewhere, even if it's only spectacle. (I once saw a medicine for stomach upsets sold by dressing actors up as gherkins, peppers, onions, rich cheese and some of the other foods that are delicious to eat but upsetting afterwards.) Sometimes you may be attacked for using what is called 'borrowed interest', but if a product is totally uninteresting, and plenty are, then even 'borrowed interest' is better than no interest at all.

In the last analysis, you know yourself whether an ad is boring; if you are, as I recommend, your own sternest critic, you will decide, however weary you feel, that it's worth one last try. I know it's easy to say 'boring', but when you look at the number of ads around that really *are*, don't you wish some creative people tried harder?

I will end with a warning. There really is nothing more tedious than a creative team defending an ad that isn't worth the paper it's written on. I have seen it many times, and as the tempers rise and the language degenerates, do try and remember, if you are an account person, that rash defences are often born of insecurity. A creative person has willingly put himself in the engine room of the agency and there can be times when he can't have an idea at any price. I council firmness but kindness. And to creative people who see their best work end up in the wastepaper basket, there are two things you can do. Rescue some of it and take it to a creative director you respect. If he offers you a job, take it, because you are in the wrong agency and your talent is being wasted. If you don't want to move, but still can't get your ads through the system, remember they are only ads. And read Chapter 14.

Chapter 13

HOW TO PRESENT YOUR WORK

I believe in one basic rule in presenting creative work to
clients: the presentation should be made by the people who
did the work. This may not always be possible. Sometimes the
people who made the ads might not want to present them.
Sometimes they are so slow on their feet that it takes a more
nimble tongue and quicker wit to 'sell' the work to a client.
Sometimes it may be agency policy to divorce the creative
department completely from the client. There are two
reasons for this: first, the creative people may be so close
to the work that they cannot acknowledge it has any defects
at all, so become aggressive if the meeting does not go well.
Second, there may be times when a client gets attached to a
creative team, which can be embarrassing for an agency if that
team decides to go elsewhere: the client may decide he wants
to follow them. There is one very successful agency in London
where the creative people never present the work, yet some
might say that the same agency owns some of the most
talented creative people around. Notwithstanding the
exceptions, I stick by my first assertion. If you made the ad
then you should present it.

Why? Because when you made the ad you learned all about
the product and all about the customers, so you know
exactly why you did it the way you did and can explain

those reasons at the meeting. But more important, you have got to face the man whose money you are spending and defend your work. If you haven't done your best then you will have to take the flack for it. You can't hide behind some hapless executive while the client pounds him for missing some of the best selling features of his product. Moreover, since you are originators, you are also very committed to your work and consequently should be able to put it in its best light. Finally, if the work is turned down, you will know why it was turned down, how it was turned down, and you will have no one to blame for the rejection but yourself.

This is not to say I think that account people don't put their hearts into selling good work. Far from it. I once worked with a very senior account person who, if he was happy with a campaign and convinced it would do its job, would go to the wall to defend it. He took stands at meetings at which I was present that were far more extreme than I would have taken myself. Where I would have compromised he was adamant, and nine times out of ten he got away with it. Certainly, it was a pleasure to work for him, since his firm commitment made it incumbent on me to turn out the very best possible job.

Use your main advantage

Whenever you walk into a client presentation you should remember that, until the campaign has been shown, you are in a highly advantageous position. There is no time in the client-agency relationship when you have so much of the client's rapt and undivided attention. He wants to see the creative work, he wants to be surprised, he hopes he will also be convinced ads are right, and he is looking forward to advertisements that excite him. Moreover you are talking about the one subject most dear to him — the product he has spent his career making and selling.

All the time he is listening to the preamble, he is thinking about the work. Charts are nice, media plans are nice, research findings can be fascinating; but nothing is more 'grabby' than actually being introduced to the theme of a new campaign and being shown how it develops into a series of advertisements, each building on a different aspect of the product, or presenting the proposition in a slightly different way to emphasise one feature, then another, until the whole product personality has evolved. At this time you should have the client in the palm of your hand and he will look at your layouts, race ahead of you to read your headlines and assimilate your argument for the product, and only in exceptional circumstances interrupt the flow of your presentation.

First impressions matter

There is a lot to be learned from this simple fact. First, your advertisements should look good. I'm not suggesting that you typeset headlines, take experimental photographs and cover the lot with acetate and glossy masking paper. Very often those refinements are used to disguise the fact that the work is poor.

But I am suggesting that if you have a good idea, see that the presentation does it justice. Regardless how many times clients tell you they can 'read' scamps, or that they only want to see your basic thoughts, you simply cannot produce basic thoughts in a client presentation, you have to come up with the final concept; otherwise it's back to base and you're not having a presentation at all, you're having a progress meeting. And progress meetings demontrate only one thing: unless you've got a finished idea, you haven't made much progress.

You may have whole pages to work in, or you may have smaller spaces; it's never a bad idea to make the ads you pin on the presentation room wall bigger than they will appear in the publication. Acknowledge the fact in your opening sentence by all means, but point out that, since the client is sitting at the boardroom table and the ad is probably 15 feet away from him, the large size is partly to help communicate the idea at that distance.

Naked into the conference

If you are producing an idea for a film or a television
commercial, then always draw up a storyboard. Going into a
presentation with only a typewritten script is like going
naked to the conference chamber. I know there are arguments
which say it's better to act out your commercial rather than
draw it. I know it has been said that if you show a woman
with blonde hair on the storyboard the client will want the
model in the commercial to have just that hue in her own
hair. This is not just naive, it underestimates the intelligence
of the client; if you do think your man is going to react like
that then make it perfectly clear that he is looking at a still
drawing, not a piece of live film. A storyboard indicates
intent but is never to be interpreted literally. A script is
merely words and, although you are perfectly clear what
they mean, you're going to have to be a communications
wizard to get what you 'see' in a script to be the same thing
as clients 'see'. A storyboard is the one occasion when you
can be sure that twelve pictures are worth twelve thousand
words.

Moreover, when you draw storyboards, you give your work
weight. I know that no first-division agency should have to
provide a client with evidence that it has done work. But a
storyboard *is* evidence that you have done work, more work
than appears on a single typewritten sheet, and evidence
helps, even is it's not needed to prove your case. Finally,
films and commercials are to do with *pictures;* how can you
hope to show them in any light at all if you don't *use*
pictures? Bill Bernbach, the best-known copywriter of them
all, says: 'How can you storyboard a smile?'. There's no
answer to that. But there is another question: 'How can you
write a smile in a TV script?'. I'll put my money on a
professional storyboard artist to communicate the intention
quicker.

I have little experience of making test commercials. I've
done it and it's expensive and rarely achieves the effect you
want, because you can't buy the right artists or the right
director and, until recently, you couldn't edit very
efficiently on videotape. I'm not sold on the need to make

test commercials: for one thing they only last half-a-minute and the client needs something he can look at for a lot longer than that and, if necessary, take away in his briefcase afterwards. So I don't advocate going to all this time, trouble and expense; it's simply not worth it. But it is worth doing storyboards. I would never ask any creative team to present a commercial without them.

Horses for courses

So the first basic principle in presentation is to arm yourself with the right creative ammunition. Large, well drawn concepts for Press ads and the same large well drawn storyboards of the key frames of your film. There are times when it helps to have the whole storyboard up on your easel at once, and other times when it's best to put the key frames a picture at a time. You will have to decide which method is appropriate for the commercial you have to show; content is all.

If you are a junior copywriter in an agency which has a set formula for presenting creative work, and that formula does not follow the one I have outlined here, then you will obviously have to work to the system that operates at your place. If the agency policy is to keep you away from the client, then you'll have to pass your work over to someone else. If it's your agency's practice to present scripts, rather than storyboards, then you'll have to abide by the rules. In that situation, there's no profit in kicking against the pricks. All I would say is that when you get into a place that allows you to make your own decisions on matters of presentation, you'll find my advice will pay dividends.

So much for arming yourself with the material you have to present. Now a word about the speech you are going to make. Unless you are highly experienced in the business it won't do you any harm to make a few notes on what you want to say. What matters is not that you may forget to make some of the points in your sales story, but that you might not make them in the right order. Your argument should have a simplicity and a logic that is irrefutable, and logic is mostly a matter of the order in which you make your proposition. I'm not suggesting you need a rehearsal every time you prepare for a presentation — though if it is a vitally important one then that may not be amiss — but simply that you should muster a logical case for what you want to say and support your thesis with as many facts as are relevant.

You have one invaluable aid in creative presentations, apart from the fact that you have the client's undivided attention, and that is 'the creative strategy'. The following story may illustrate how crucial the strategy can be. I once made a very important advertising campaign for a client who was launching a new product. As luck would have it, on the day of the presentation, I was struck down with flu, so my art director — no slouch in presentations — had to take on the job instead. We picked a bad time of the week, Friday afternoon, and we were in the middle of a heat wave.

Result: a lost campaign, not through anybody's fault but through force of circumstance. The agency made a brave decision — to re-present the work a week or so later, taking into account the client's comments and giving due consideration to his objections, which, in my view, were primarily the result of imprecise thinking. Now the decision to re-present is a difficult one at any time, and the chances of success are around 100-to-1 against. But we were sure we had a good campaign and equally sure that it was a sound (not to say imaginative) interpretation of the strategy.

The second meeting with the client began in a tense atmosphere, but I had decided several days before that it was no part of my job to 'sell' the client a campaign he had rejected. It was very much part of my job to get him to agree we were working to the right strategy.'After all, both agency and client had worked to put it together; all we had to decide was that we'd done the job right, and no circumstance had arisen to force a change. I started my talk by admitting the situation the agency was in; I was not, I said, going to present a new advertising campaign. But I also emphasised that I was not going to try and make the client accept the campaign he had already seen. What I wanted to do was examine the suggestions made at the previous presentation and see whether they could and should be integrated into the strategy. I said at the outset: 'Mr Client, *there is always another campaign'*.

No 'psychobabble', please

So we went through our business reasoning, point by point. I had a list of objections that the client had raised and we examined each of those carefully to see whether there was a place for any of them in the argument we wanted to put to our audience. I was coldly logical, careful to speak simply and avoid jargon, and I used phrases that my wife would have understood if I had been putting the case for the product to her. And I raised the objections to the argument I thought she would raise and then, whenever possible, overcame them with advantages that stemmed from the product and had been outlined in the creative strategy.

The client, since he realised he was not going to be steam-rollered into buying any creative work, was prepared to listen. In not too long a time, we agreed that the thinking outlined in the strategy was sound and that sensible arguments against it could be refuted sensibly. It was only at this point that I turned to the creative work. Again I asked the client only to decide if the ads lived up to the thinking behind the strategy, and I went through the headline and copy claims point by point, cross-checking against the strategy to see that nothing had been missed, nothing understated and, equally important, nothing overstated. Because the strategy was demonstrably right, it was a reasonably simple job to demonstrate that the ads were right. They were not the only way to skin the cat (and I was careful to make that point too); but they were a highly professional interpretation of a sound selling proposition, had not been arrived at lightly and, if we were to go back to the drawing board, it wasn't because we were off strategy, but because the client — entirely within his rights — simply didn't like the work.

In meetings of this kind it is important to admit that you may not be 100 per cent right; you shouldn't expect to win every point in every argument; clients are very rarely fools and unless you have done a great deal of homework they probably know more about the product and certainly more about the manufacturing and distribution problems than you. There is a post-script to this story. When the advertisements finally ran, they pushed the clients product to number-one in the market. And although he no longer works with the product in question, nor I with the agency in question, we still greet each other on christian name terms.

Think like a creative person, talk like an accountant

You can take it from me that any attempt to point out the beauty, 'creativity' or impact of the ads would have been quite useless. No client is impressed with those qualities if he doesn't like the big idea. But once the suspicion of high pressure salesmanship has been set at rest, and you have the client's ear, business sense normally prevails. You can't expect a client to recognise a brilliant advertising campaign when he sees it (what is brilliant, anyway? What one man loves another won't buy at any price), and it's not his job to know good work when he sees it.

It's your job to convince him that the work is good and you won't do that simply by declaring 'Look at this; isn't it great?'. That is why it is vital that the creative team are involved when the strategy is written and that they understand it and agree with it. And also that they look on it not as a restriction of their imagination, but as a discipline that will point them in the only direction in which good solutions are to be found. So the moral is this: you should go into a client presentation determined to *prove that the ads are 'on strategy'*. And the imagination and craft with which they interpret that strategy should speak for themselves. Never go to the wall over a campaign; it isn't worth it, and anyway, in the last analysis, the client has the right to say 'I don't like it'. But by all means do your utmost to defend the strategy. That is easier because the client has had a major say in devising it and moreover, if the strategy is correct, you can always find another way to interpret it. (I shall have more to say about the idea that there is always another campaign in Chapter 14.)

Thinking while you listen

When you have made your presentation and the ads are on
the wall waiting for the client's comments, then is the time
you have to be able to think on your feet. First presentations
should be concerned with concepts; it's rarely a good idea
to get down to discussing the body text at this early stage.
Get your pictures and headlines agreed, show that each
different ad is making a single point in the selling price and
that, together, the ads make up an attractive and coherent
personality for the product. Since the work you have done
probably took several weeks to perfect and each ad has been
given several 'overnight tests', you will have already mustered
your reasons for why you did what you did. The time to
expand on them is if you have to face heavy criticism; but
be careful to deal with your client in an attitude of
friendliness. Be prepared to listen and, if it doesn't hurt the
campaign, within reason to agree. I cannot emphasise too
strongly that the best defence is common-sense and logic. The
worst situation to be in is defending an ad for emotional
reasons or because, at that moment, you can't think of
another way of doing it. This is not a plea for compromise.
I am very wary of the desire to accommodate every point the
client makes as soon as he makes it, because often he is
simply asking questions to find out whether you have thought
the business through and found the right answers.

Surprise, surprise

A client who cross-examines you in a presentation can soon
fathom how much thinking you have done on the campaign
and how deeply you are committed to the ads. He can also
tell very quickly if you are defending work for the wrong
reasons, and if you are not as confident of your recommendations as you would like to appear. Vibes come over in client
meetings; the rights and wrongs of an argument will soon
become apparent if discussions are held in an atmosphere of
businesslike common-sense, with no allowances made for
creative temperament. (Which is not to say the client

shouldn't make allowances for unexpected turns of phrase in headlines and surprises in the ads.) If I come out of a presentation without having surprised the client with my creative work, I think I've failed.

Leave at the right time

Let us say that at the end of the presentation the client has given a tentative 'yes' and the ads seem to have jumped the first hurdle on their way to the medium in which they'll appear. That's the time to stop. A highly successful account person I know puts the situation in six words: 'Make the sale. And get out.' Once the decision to accept the work has been made, any further discussion is generally unprofitable. People are tired, get bogged down in unimportant details, and can often forget the original intent of the work. The initial surprise of seeing the ads has gone, the client's attention is no longer yours for the asking, and prolonged discussion simply raises doubts and second thoughts. Remember, the first impression is the important thing: the average reader will give your ad about 1½ seconds, so there's little to be gained by poring over work for 1½ hours. Make sure you know what you and the client agree on, and what you disagree on, and the next steps to take. Then go, man, go.

Chapter 14

HOW TO LIVE WITH A DEAD CAMPAIGN

In theory, there should be only three reasons for a client to
reject a campaign:
1   It's not 'on strategy'.
2   Events have overtaken it.
3   It's been done before.
In practice we can add a fourth reason which, although it may
seem irrational, is, in my view, perfectly acceptable.
4   The client doesn't like it.
As far as the first reason is concerned — the campaign which
doesn't give a correct interpretation of the strategy — this
should have been killed in the creative director's office, or
certainly a long time before it got presented to the client.
There is absolutely no value in the agency people and the
client agreeing on a strategy if the creative people don't
follow it. And consequently, there is no way to defend it
during a presentation, and quite rightly; it ought to be killed
there and then.

If events overtake your campaign, the fault can lie in several
places; one is with the client, since he may not have appraised
the agency of the new situation, another is with the account
people, who may have known that something had happened,
but either didn't pass on the information to the writer and
art director, or assumed that it would make no difference.

If the campaign has been done before, either by your own client, or by a competitor, again it should die, or the client will simply be spending his money to promote someone else's products. But it can often happen that nobody knows of the existence of the other campaign (it is not unknown for two agencies to produce similar advertisements, almost simultaneously), in which case you have to accept the fact that duplication can happen.

You are best advised to give up your version and start again; if two people think of the same idea at the same time, there is a likelihood that it's a pretty obvious idea, and you will be the stronger of the two agencies if you volunteer to rethink. A client shouldn't be too hard on his agency if it does produce work similar to someone else — provided he is sure he is dealing with a first-division agency. Creative people in the best shops strongly dislike 'cribbing' and are far too conscientious to present another agency's thinking as their own.

The illogical 'no'

Which brings us to the fourth reason — the client doesn't like it. I may have surprised you when I said I felt this reason to be acceptable. I believe this because, in the last analysis, the client is paying the bill and should not be forced into buying a product he doesn't feel happy with — you would never buy anything you didn't like. But more than this, even if a clever account person does persuade the client to accept work which he dislikes, and even if that work appears in the media, the client will always have a deep-down feeling he has been pressurised, and that is the first step to looking for a new agency. One thing is virtually certain: even if the work runs for a year, it will certainly be killed at the end of that time anyway (disappointed clients can be very persistent) unless it has proved, beyond any doubt, to be effective.

If your client does say 'no' and cannot articulate his reasons, some agencies offer to 'research' the campaign to prove that it is right. The proper place for research, however, is before the campaign has been written. That way all the findings, based on only the proposition, can be included in the finished work. Campaigns researched after they have been done are more often than not on a hiding to nothing (we all know how research groups like to set themselves up as advertising judges). And anyway, even if everything does go the way the agency wants, if I were a client and I hated the work, I would politely suggest that the agency stuff the research findings. So what should the disappointed creative person do? What certainly *doesn't* help is to blow your top. I have done it myself after a disasterous presentation, and it is simply sound and fury, signifying nothing.

Oh, it's you again!

You must always remember that you are going to have to meet the client again. You are going to have to present him with a second campaign. If you prove yourself insensitive to his feelings, and seemingly unable to accept his views, he will only give you a hard time second time round. The best relationships between creative people and a client is that of 'friends'. You have to show that you understand his business problems, his likes and dislikes and his 'intuitive' feelings on how his product should be promoted. He may never be able to produce a campaign himself, but do remember he has had the entrepreneurial skills to devise and manufacture a product, secure distribution for it, and find enough money to advertise it. Not many genuine entrepreneurs are clowns; they very often have a knack of being able to sell tuppeny apples for threepence, which is a skill most copywriters could well do with. So, above all, try to retain a good relationship with your client, and convince him that you are on his side and that you both want the best possible advertising for the product. Some creative people are in the unhappy position of having earned themselves reputations for being bolshy; in the final event this can only lead to the client telling the agency that he wants a completely new group to work on his account.

Listen to what he means

The most positive thing you can do is spend time talking with the client, face to face. If possible, try not to let the account people get in the way. If you listen carefully to what your man says, and then take out of the meeting what he actually means (which are very rarely one and the same thing) you will be in a better position to have a second go. I have known a time when I did work for a client which was rejected not once, but three times; finally I sat down and had a real heart-to-heart with him, not in an atmosphere of rancour but of co-operation. At the end of that chat, what he wanted was crystal clear, and then my only responsibility was to put it down on paper in a way that was truly professional. Don't get me wrong; I'm not saying give the client what he *says* he wants; instead listen to what he says and use your skill and experience to turn those thoughts into good advertisements.

Clients rarely know how to make good ads. But they are not without ideas on what sells their product, and many of them may have been out on the road actually doing the selling, so take care before you reject what they have learned from that experience.

Clients lose sleep too

At the same time, it is not uncommon for clients to be so close to their products that they can't separate sales points from simple information. They want you to understand the sleepless nights they have had thinking about the product in all its facets and this can frequently get them bogged down in detail. They ask to have every single advantage in the headline repeated in the sub-heading, and reiterated throughout the body copy. You can combat this if you remember two things. First, the experience of the tyre manufacturer who, although he had a terrific number of sales points to make, honed them down to one main thought: safety. Always try to make an ad which concentrates at first on a main thought. Secondly, there is a little rhyme which will help you and your client to see details more clearly:

Oh tell me this, and tell me true
Or else, my love, to hell with you,
Less how the product came to be
And more for what it does for me.

Sad to say, the customer does not want to know the history of
the product and all the problems the client had before he
perfected it. He wants to know what's in it for him. Say that
little ditty to your client (nicely, of course) and it will help
you to make it clear to him the importance of promise,
promise and more promise, which is (as you've probably
heard a million times) the soul of an advertisement.

Right, your campaign has been killed, but your relationship
with the client hasn't, in fact if you've done your talking well
it's on a better footing than it ever has been and you are beginning to get a 'feel' of his expectations (and indeed his limita-
tions). What's the next move?

New doesn't mean once more with feeling

Throw out of your mind all the thoughts of the first campaign.
I don't mean forget the market background, far from it. All
the time spent finding out facts about the product, the buyer
and the market is time very well invested and it will pay you
dividends now. But don't try and produce the same creative
work with different words, because if the client didn't like the
proposition first time round, he surely won't like the same
idea expressed differently. And anyway, if you're any good,
you found the best words to use for your first campaign. You
must look for a new idea. How?

Every good agency has one or two people in the creative
department who don't mind helping. The first person is, of
course, the creative director, and if he is any good at all, he
will have brought his mind to bear on your problem and be
able to make some suggestions, even if they are only tentative
and not formed into a campaign idea. But go to all the senior
people in the creative department and talk things over. Listen
to people who are positive. It may be that this is your first
campaign on a product which has been transferred to you

from another group. Go to the people who previously did the good work; they will not mind you picking their brains; if they have the right attitude to our business they should be flattered. But if you meet someone who tells you not to be surprised that your work has been turned down, and goes on to talk about what a rotten product you've got and what a difficult company you have to deal with, the best thing to do is switch off or change the subject. All they are trying to do is make excuses for shoddy work *they've* done; complaints about products and clients can only dishearten you and since you are going to have to go into the arena a second time you would be well advised to enter with good grace. Seek out the good thinkers in your agency, people not afraid to make suggestions on how to approach the problem, and even if they don't actually have an idea for you, they may say a sentence or two which sets you thinking on a new line.

Talk to the media people

Take a fresh look at the media you are using and, if it's at all practical, change it. Good advice for every creative person is to have a special buddy in the media department.

You get hold of him and tell him who you want to talk to and how much money you've got to spend. Say the target audience is young girls, aged 16-24, and the campaign you've had rejected used whole pages in the right women's magazines. He might suggest that you think about a cinema film — cinema reaches the same age group. Or he may have news of a different kind of space the magazines are promoting at that time, say the mini-page, or four quarter-pages across the spread. Any suggestion of a different way to reach the audience can be very helpful when you are considering a new approach to creative work. If you're in the London area only, think about the free-sheets — those give-away magazines all the secretaries are offered at the main line and underground stations. The cost is so low you could take really dominant spaces here. But I don't want to suggest alternative media, simply impress upon you the help a good media man can provide. If he becomes interested in the creative job and understands that media buying is really part of the creative function, he will never leave you without at least having stimulated your mind as to possible new ways to approach your campaign. I will go further and say you should never produce any major campaign without first having a long chat with someone in the media department. I have always been lucky enough to strike up a relationship with one particular guy who never minds using his imagination and isn't mesmerised by cost-per-thousands. If you can't find a good friend among the media people, at least you can get together with the planners on each of your accounts as the opportunities arise.

Don't get whipped by the clock

So you have talked the situation over with the creative director, you have walked around picking the best brains available and you have had a pow-wow with the media guys. Your next problem will probably be time. Since your first campaign was produced to meet copy dates, it's likely that these will not be far away. Worries about deadlines never help you do good work. So, if possible you should try and get extensions on your first copy dates; it might even not do too much harm if the launch date is postponed for a few days to ensure the creative work is right. If you spend half-a-million pounds on a second-rate campaign, you won't have proved a great deal just by launching on the day planned.

Clients understand this too, and account people certainly should by sympathetic. I'm not saying ask for more time on principle; but I am saying it's never good to be whipped by the clock. Parkinson's law certainly applies in creative departments, as it does in any office, and I know a number of good creative people who are at their best when the pressure is on. But if lack of time worries you, then it is a handicap the rest of the agency should do their utmost to remove. The man with the most authority to help here is the creative director, so if deadlines are ridiculous, put your case to him.

Remember Robert-the-Bruce

Now, a word of warning. There can be a temptation, especially amongst those creative people who have had little experience in the business, to try less hard second time around. I'm not saying it applies to everyone, but the disappointment of a rejected campaign can linger for days and kill enthusiasm. If you give in and produce second-rate work, you'll be asking for trouble. The creative director should kick you around the building, but you will also upset your account people and you will get no sympathy whatsoever from the experienced creative people who will have been in your situation and *worked* to get out of it. But let us for a moment suppose that you *do* manage to get some second-rate ad through the system. No one will be sorrier than yourself in the days to come when the proofs roll off the presses or the commercial appears and you blush every time someone puts your name to it. What's worse, all the efforts you put into the first campaign, and the tears you shed over the second, will never show in the ads that finally appear. To the great British Public, not to mention your co-workers in the trade, it will look like just another low-class job where nobody tried hard enough. And that is precisely what it will be. Whenever a creative person opens his portfolio and shows me a poor ad, but hurries on to tell me I should have seen the original (but the client didn't like it!), I know exactly what to think.

There is another temptation: to quit! You decide you're not appreciated in your present agency so you'll go somewhere else.

You either ring up your favourite head-hunter and tell him you're looking, or you start to scan the appointments pages of the trade press. This state of affairs — quite funny when you read about it, but believe me it really happens — can go on until you get too high up to run away; is it an answer? In my experience, not really since it is a fact of life that problems you turn your back on have this unfortunate knack of turning up again from another direction. And not just in agency life. I am sure there are plenty of clients who think twice about swopping agencies (and hence bolshy

creative people) because the devil they know is better than
the devil they haven't met yet. Certainly I am sure that the
client whose expectations you know is 20 times better than
the client whose expectations *you* haven't had to meet yet.
This is not to say you have to become a punch bag, but
hopefully you're too intelligent for that anyway. Move on
when the right opportunity presents itself by all means, but
there's no profit in changing agencies as an escape route.
The number of people who change their jobs for the right
reasons is small in any business, but you can do yourself a
big favour if you look very carefully before you leap. There
is a very strong possibility — I'd say you can almost bet on
it — that the first account you have to work on at your new
place will present you with the same kind of problems you
refused to face at your old place. And this isn't the fault of
advertising agencies, it's the very nature of business — any
business, you might say of life itself.

An idea to remember

So, to summarise: don't burn your boats with the client;
listen carefully to what he has to say; fillet the meat out of
his suggestions; talk with your creative director and the other
helpful creative people you have around; reconsider your
choice of media; never try to regurgitate your old work; do
your utmost to see you have enough time; don't give up and
produce poor work; and don't take the easy route to another
agency. Try, if you can, to bear this next thought in mind.
It is not a popular idea, and there are some places where they
don't like it to get around for fear the client will start
whipping the agency. But it is perfectly true, and if you
can weave it into your working philosopy you will find you
walk with a lighter step.
    The thought is this: *there is always another campaign.*
I could make it stronger and say there is always another
campaign inside you, but as sure as God made little fishes, if
you can't think of it, someone else in or outside your agency
certainly can. So be professional about it; that is the truth of
this whole situation; accept it and live up to it and no one will
ever get the better of you.

Which brings me to some thoughts on what a professional creative person should be. I have a view, as this book testifies, that the true advertising writer is one who has taken time and trouble to learn his skills. Not just through practice, but through study. By this I don't advocate that you spend long years in college. I would never have a creative person spend more than one scholastic year getting the foundations of his craft, and if he can spend that year going round the other departments in an agency rather than at college, so much the better. When you get to the stage where you are making and presenting big campaigns for major clients (and I don't see this happening until several years after you first start as a copywriter) then your behaviour should be such that can only win you respect in the eyes of your client. He should be able to view you with the same confidence and expect to hear you speak with the same authority as the marketing man with his computer print-outs and the research man with his depth interviews. You should have a grasp of the market situation on a par with the account person who makes the selling recommendations; put in the venacular, that means you should understand buying and selling. You buy cheap, you put labour into the product, and you sell at the best price the market will bear. And you do that for one reason only: to make a profit. You should not see yourself as a frustrated poet or novelist who prostitutes his art by writing copy. Write poetry by all means, but put the same craft into your ads; earn your living honestly. Realise that your function is to get people to spend and help your client to earn his living and keep his factories busy and his employees rich.

Accept that you are in the engine room of the agency, making the only product the public will see, and never be afraid to roll your sleeves up and get sweaty. Some people will say you work in an ivory tower, but this is no more true of you than it is of your client who also works in an office with pleasant furniture and may be a carpet on the floor, yet has to keep his job by making goods that the public want. Ivory tower critics invariably live in ivory towers themselves; that's where they get the idea from. Since you are part of the cycle of production, there is no place in your job for temperament or displays of heavy sighing. Shout and scream in your own office by all means, set fire to the layouts, rush home, kick the dog and beat the wife. That's expected from creative people — just don't do it where anyone else has to suffer it.

If you have decided you want to be a creative person behave so that you can be justly proud of the work you do, whether it's the first campaign for the product or (God forbid) the fourth. A true test is whether you are pleased to have your name connected with it if it should ever come under discussion. If you always make good ads, you won't just have an enviable portfolio to show. You will have clients who look forward to presentations from you and are keen to buy your work if they possibly can. You will have account people who ask your opinion on matters of marketing, expect you to make a major contribution to any strategy you draw up together, and want to have you working for their clients. Because you are professional, and are recognised as such, you will soon be able to command a good salary, which will increase just so long as you produce outstanding creative work. And if all this is true, it need not be too long before you begin to win advertising awards and earn yourself a name. Love, security, wealth and recognition. What else is there?

INDEX

The letter-by-letter system of alphabetisation has been
adopted. The principal entries within the index are four:
'Advertising' relating to the various aspects of advertisements;
'Copywriting' which deals with the people creating the
advertisement; 'Media' concerning getting the advertisement
across; and 'Job' which covers the copywriter himself.

Ability, assessing your own, *see
    under* Job, attributes of
    a copywriter's
Account people, scope of, 1-2
Accounts:
    duties of man handling, 2, 11
    how to improve a client's,
        8-9
    keeping a list of all, 6
    see also Client
Advertising:
    black and white or colour, 21
    body content, 127-8
    content matters more than
        style, 28
    customer, visualising the
        typical, 24-5
    dead campaigns, 145-55:

another campaign concept,
    153-5
consult others, 149-50
deadline extensions, 151
ditty to remember, 149
reasons for rejection, 145
Robert-the-Bruce line,
    152-3
second presentations, 147
seek media's advice, 150
when client dislikes it,
    146-7
do's and don'ts, 28
how long ought it to be?, 128
how to start a new assignment,
    20-1
message: *What to say* not *How
    to say*, 39-50

buyer, aim at what interests
the, 46
concentrate on fact finding,
50
create effect by saying
something effective, 44
Ryvita campaign, example
of, 45-9
sell rather than impress, 40
strategy, planning your,
40-1, 49
surprise element, 48
talk sense using correct
tone, 43
who are you aiming at?, 42
worry, avoidance of, 49
outline sketch, 27
purpose of, 39
'spot' colours, 21
techniques of, see Techniques
of advertising
telling the reader something
new, 23
the seven vital points of, 116-
21
two categories of only, 30-8
those with something to
say, 31-3
when there is nothing to
say, 33-8
where they appear, 30
working to actual size, 27
work of an advertiser, see Job,
attributes of a
copywriter's
see also under Housewife; Job,
attributes of a copy-
writer's; Television under
Media
'Ad-y-ism', critics of, 131-2
Animation in films, 90
Anxiety-busting, 20, 49, 115, 151
Artwork, what it involves, 3, 5
Attention-rousers, 58-9, 59-66
see also Housewife; Reader
Ayds Slimming Toffee campaign,
68

Babies and women's attention,
106
Beanz Meanz Heinz campaign,
36-7
Beauty and women's attention,
111-13
Before and after technique, 67-8
Bleeding, problem of, 21
Buzz words, 79

Campaigns, 36, 68
see also Advertising; Beanz
Meanz Heinz; Copy-
writing; Ryvita;
Techniques of
advertising
Campaigns, dead, see under
Advertising
Captions, 56-7
Cartoons, using strip, 92
Challenge as a basis for
advertising technique, 76
Character, inventing a, 70
Charts, 57
Christenings and women's
attention, 106
Clients:
discovering needs of, 1-2
four reasons for rejection,
145-6
including the, in advertising,
70-1
keep a list of all, 6
likely criticisms of, 125-34
see also Presenting your work
under Job, attributes of
a copywriter's
presentation of work to,
135-44
see also Dead campaigns under
Advertising
see also Accounts
Commercials, see Television under
Media
Comparison technique, 72-5
Competitors:

testimonials from, technique
of using, 81
using the same word as,
129-30
Contests technique, 80
Copywriting:
aims of this study in, xi-xii
equipment needed, 5-6
first day in the office, 1-9:
accounts, how to improve
₁your client', 8-9
artworkers, 3, 5
cinema, what can be
learned at, 7-8
client accounts, 1-2, 6
creativity, who are those
with?, 3-4
director, creative, *see under*
Director
four types of persons
involved, 1-3
illustrators, 4-5
library, making use of, 6-7
media, what is available,
2
paste-up artists, 5
photographs, 2
producers, TV and film, 3-4
production people, 2
re-touching process, 2
Thesaurus, Roget's, 6
tools required, 5-7
transparencies, 2
typewriters, 6
typographers, importance of,
4
typography, 4-5
visiting the agency cinema,
7-8
habits, adopting good, 19-29:
anxiety-busting, 20
bleeding and gutter
problems, 21
customer, visualising the
typical, 24-5
discrimination, developing
the art of, 26
doing the office rounds
dialy, 19
do's and don'ts, 28
factory visits, 22-3
familiarity with product,
24
how to start a new assignment, 20-1
market research, 24-5
outline sketch, 27
seeking unbiassed opinion,
24
site visits, 22-3
studying the journal
concerned, 20-2
target audience, 25
team-work, developing the
art of, 25-6
tell the reader something
new, 23
working to actual size, 27
work on content, not
style, 28
what sort of person is good at,
154-5
see also Job, attributes of a
copywriter's; Media;
Techniques of
advertising
Coupon campaigns, 107-8
Creative Advertising (Bernstein),
26, 93
Creativity, *see* Director, creative
Criticisms likely to be encountered,
125-34
Customer, visualising the typical,
24-5
Cut-outs, 54

'Day', use of word, in
advertising, 90
Dead campaigns, *see under*
Advertising
Deadlines, 115, 151
Demonstrations, 87
on TV, 97-8
Diagrams, 57

Dictionaries, 6, 39, 87
Director, creative:
  first meeting with, 5
  helping with dead campaign,
    149-150, 151
  his work:
    agency stands or falls by,
      10-12
    attributes, 12-13
    delegation by, 17
    discipline, responsible for,
      14
    duties of, 13-14
    firing staff, 17
    hiring staff, 15
    'hot-shops', 18
    knowing what is going on,
      16-17
    necessity for discrimination,
      25-6
    spiking without destroying
      further creativity, 17
    staff control, 15
    successor, having in mind
      a, 16
    taking stick, ability for,
      17-18

Economy sizes, 110-11
Equipment needed, 5-6

Factory visits and observation,
  22-3
Fashion play, 106-7, 112
  see also under Housewife
Feminine angle, see Housewife
Films, see Television and films
  under Media
Free samples, 108-9
Free-sheets, 150

Girls, see Housewife
Graphs, 57
Guarantee, advertising
  incorporating, 76

Headlines, should there be
  questions in?, 130

Heinz Beanz, 36-7
Housewife, talking to the,
  103-13:
  babies, 106
  beauty, 111-13
  certain exceptions do not
    involve, 103
  christenings, 106
  coupons, 107-8
  economy sizes, 110-11
  facts and information is what
    she wants, 105
  fashion play, 106-7, 112
  free samples, 108-9
  key attractions, 111
  limited offers to be explicit,
    110
  recipes, 107
  savings on housekeeping, 111
  shops, sales in the, 110
  steal techniques, 106
  truthful claims are a must,
    105
  value for money, 110-11
  weddings, 106
  what interests her, 106
  what NOT to leave out, 113
  when the answer is: 'You
    must be joking', scrap
    it, 105, 112
'How' technique, 61-2, 66
Hunger for work, having an
  appetite for, 44-15

Ideas for factory or site visits,
  22-3
Illustrators, 4-5
Inch War, see Ryvita

Jingles, 100
Job, attributes of a copywriter's:
  defending your work, 123-34:
    criticisms to be en-
      countered, 125-34
    discarding work, 123
    do not rely on body copy,
      127-8

face-to-face with client,
125-6
facing the plans board, 125
in TV work try it without
sound, 126-7
showing the boss, 124-5
three campaigns a year is
good going, 123
what to expect, 125-34:
judging your own work, 114-
22:
deadlines, 115
seven vital points, 116-21:
presenting your work to
client, 125-44:
answering objections, 141-2
conference, what to be
ready for at, 138-9
cut psychotic babble, 141-
2
do it yourself, 135-6
first impressions,
importance of, 137
have ready the surprise
element, 143-4
re-presentation later on,
140
storyboards, 138-9
strategy, 140-2
talk like an accountant,
142-3
think as you listen, 143
think creatively, 142-3
use your main advantage
to advantage, 135-7
when to get up and go,
144
your speech, 139-41

Key words in advertising, 79,
111

Ladies, see Housewife
Library, making use of, 6-7
Limited offers to be explicit,
110

Magazines, see under Media;
Techniques of
advertising
Market research, time well
spent on, 24-5
Media:
films:
advertising by making,
87-90
clients' pre-view of, 138-9
for television, 93-102
magazines, 2, 30
and the housewife, 106-7
bleeding and gutter
problems, 21
criticism of work for, 131
or 'Box', 93-4, 96, 102
study of back numbers
and editorial matter,
20-2
watch the correspondence
columns, 20-1
see also under Housewife
media people:
help from, with dead
campaign, 150-1
list of typical kinds of
advertisements for, 30
scope of, 2, 11
see also under Housewife
newspapers, 2, 30
or 'Box', 93-4, 96, 102
see also under Housewife
posters, 2, 30
see also under Housewife
radio, 2, 30
television:
'Box' or press, 93-4, 96,
102
clients' pre-view of, 138-9
commercials by personal
presentation, 99
demonstration, 97-8
dialogue rather than voice-
over, 98
dramatic pictures, 96-7
effectiveness and price are
not necessarily related, 94

jingle-jangle, 100
name catching, 98
one-shot spots, 96-7
onomatapoeics, 98
part story only is not for
    TV, 96
personalities, using well-
    known, 101
personal presentation, 99
pictures rather than words,
    96
producers, 3-4, 101-2
running time, 94-5, 101-2
script must be good and
    minimal, 94-5, 101
simplicity the essence, 95
singing jingles, 100
test commercials, 138-9
try running without sound,
    126-7
use of actors on, 64
visiting the agency's cinema,
    7-8
when it sounds stupid, sing
    it, 100
see also under Housewife
Message, see under Advertising

Newspapers, see Media; Techniques
    of advertising

Objections, countering, 125-34,
    141
Obligation discussed, 130
Onomatapoeics, 98

Paste-ups, 5
Personalities, TV, 101
Photographs, 2
    stroboscopic, 62
Place, inventing a, technique of,
    69-70
Plans Board, facing the, 125
Posters, see Media; Techniques of
    advertising
Presentation of work, see under
    Job, attributes of a
    copywriter's

Press see Newspapers; Magazines;
    (both under Media)
Product:
    changing the name of
        technique, 71-2
    essential to be familiar with,
        24
    range displays, 85
Production people, scope of, 2-3,
    11

Questions in the headline, 130
Quizes, 83-5
Quotation format of advertising,
    86-7

Radio, see Media; Techniques
    of advertising
Range displays technique, 83-5
Reaction words, 79, 111
    see also under Housewife
Reader:
    is he learning something new?,
        23
    what attracts, 58-9, 106-12
Recipes and women's attention,
    107
Rejected campaigns, see under
    Advertising (Dead)
Re-touching process, 2
Rhyming jingles, 100
Royalty, prohibition on using,
    59
Ryvita campaign, 44-9, 95, 129

Sales in the shops, 110
Samples, 108-9
Savings and women's attention,
    111
Self-assessment, see Job,
        attributes of a copy-
        writer's
Shell Make Money Campaign, 36
Shops, advertising sales in, 110
Show and Tell films, 87-8
Site visits and observation, 22-3
Slice-of-life films, 89, 105

Stand-by methods of advertising,
67-79
Standards of work, 114-22
Steal techniques, 97,106
Storyboards, 138-9
Strategy, 40-1, 49, 116, 140-2, 145
Strip cartoons, 92
Study, aims of this, xi-xii
Style no substitute for content,
28, 55-6

Target audience, 25, 42
see also Housewife
Techniques of advertising, 51-92:
  advertisement must create
    desire to take action,
    57
  attention rousers, 58-9
    see also Housewife
  captioning, 56-7
  chart-work, 57
  contests, 80
  'day', use of the word, 90
  demonstration method, 87
  facts not generalisation, 57
  films, 87-90
  'headless wonders', 54
  headline and no picture
    possibly; picture and
    no headline never, 54-5
  headline is be all and end all,
    54
  'how' technique, 61-2, 66
  lay-out, points on, 56
  one picture says more, 56
  only 1 in 150 are taken in, 52
  proven methods:
    before and after, 67-8
    changing the name of
      product, 71-2
    colliding of words, 77-8
    comparison format, 72-5
    creating a challenge, 76
    including the client, 70-1
    incorporating a guarantee,
      76
    inventing a character, 70
    inventing a place, 69-70

key words, some useful, 79
torture test format, 77
quizes, 83-5
quotation format, 86-7
range displays, 85
reader's motions when looking
  at an advertisement, 51-2
relevancy vital, 55
square pictures always, 54
strip cartoons, 92
television actors, use of, 64
testimonial from competitors,
  81
test technique, 83-5
topicality, 82
'when' technique, 66
'where' technique, 62-3, 66
'who' technique, 63-5, 66
'why' technique, 59, 61, 66
wooing the reader, 58
see also Housewife; Job,
  attributes of a copy-
  writer's; Television and
  Films *under* Media
Television, *see* Media
Testimonial from competitor
  technique, 81:
Test technique, 83-5
Thesaurus, Roget's, *see*
  Dictionaries
Tiger in the Tank Campaign,
  36
Tools for the job, 5-7
Topicality in advertising, 82
Torture test technique, 77
Trainee, advice to the, 114-15
Transparencies, 2
Trick films, 89
Truth is a must particularly for
  women, 105
Typewriter, learn to work with,
  6
Typographers, importance of,
  4-5

Unique Selling Proposition
  (USP), 33, 129

Weddings and women's attention, 106
'When' technique, 66
'Where' technique, 62-3, 66
'Who' technique, 63-5, 66
'Why' technique, 59-61, 66
Women *see* Housewife
Words:
   colliding of technique, 77-8

creating a reaction, 79, 111
criticism of competitor
   using same, 129-30
'Day', use of, 90
reactive, 79, 111
Work, *see* Job, attributes of a
   copywriter's
Worry, *see* Anxiety-busting